C0-BJF-665

Dining In—Hampton Roads
COOKBOOK

TITLES IN SERIES

Dining In—Hampton Roads

COOKBOOK

A Collection of Gourmet Recipes for Complete Meals from the
Finest Restaurants of Norfolk, Virginia Beach, and Williamsburg

JOHN GOUNARIS
and
ROBERT STANTON

Foreword by
CONGRESSMAN BILL WHITEHURST

PEANUT BUTTER PUBLISHING
SEATTLE, WASHINGTON

Cover photography: Kenneth Redding
Editor: Elaine Lotzkar
Art Director: April Ryan

Copyright © 1984 by Peanut Butter Publishing
911 Western Avenue, Suite 401 Maritime Building
Seattle, Washington 98104
All rights reserved. Printed in the United States of America

ISBN 0-89716-136-X

ACKNOWLEDGEMENTS

Dining In–Hampton Roads is the result of cooperative efforts on the part of the following nine couples, whose contributions as co-authors made this book possible.

Polly and Thomas Chisman
Susan and Peter Coe
Ann and Cliff Cutchins
Martha and Richard Davis
Jacqueline and John Gounaris
Helen Anrod Jones and Alfred B. Rollins, Jr.
Eleanor and Robert Stanton
Sally and Robert Sutton
Juanita and Eugene Walters

Grateful appreciation is extended to Elaine Lotzkar for editing the entire manuscript, to Lee Shepard for coordinating production, and to Blanche Brazzi and Judy Tate for their diligent efforts and assistance on this project.

CHILDREN'S HOSPITAL OF THE KING'S DAUGHTERS

The Children's Hospital of The King's Daughters, located in the Eastern Virginia Medical Center in Norfolk, Virginia, is the state's only general pediatric hospital and serves the major medical needs of children —from birth to adolescence—in the region. It is the hospital of choice for pediatric specialists and subspecialists, primarily because it provides the most sophisticated facility for the care of children.

Each year the tiniest babies, born too soon to unsuspecting parents, are rushed to Children's Hospital from all over the region. There they recieve a special kind of care, available only in the miracle known as the Neonatal Intensive Care Unit (NICU). Likewise, children who are injured in traffic accidents and household mishaps are brought here for critical care in an ultra-modern setting where pediatric experts work around the clock saving young lives.

Children's Hospital has evolved from The King's Daughters Clinic for mothers and sick children which was run by the women of the Norfolk City Union of The King's Daughters from 1916 until 1961. In 1961, responding to the need for far more than a clinic, The King's Daughters built and dedicated the first Children's Hospital for all children, regardless of race, religion, or ability to pay. With the help and generosity of the community, The King's Daughters expanded and remodeled the hospital in 1979.

Today, the Children's Hospital services the major health care needs of over 40,000 children a year. Adhering to the traditional philosophy of treating all children, the Hospital still accepts any child who needs the special services CHKD offers. No child is turned away because of financial circumstances.

The modern facility has 128 beds, 46 of which are intensive or otherwise special care. It also has an outstanding Ambulatory Care Center where some 36,000 children are seen in 42 specialty clinics annually.

At Children's Hospital the doctors, nurses, and technicians are especially skilled in treating children, whether drawing blood, taking x-rays, checking heartbeats, feeding, or any of the hundreds of hands-on ways children are touched each day. The uniqueness of children was uppermost in the minds of planners who created this special place for sick and injured children. The playrooms, treatment rooms, bedrooms, and waiting areas are all designed with children in mind. Special pains were taken to create a place where hospitalized children would be less frightened, less anxious, and more comfortable in general. Parents are encouraged to stay with their children. Special accommodations are made for rooming-in. Rooms are equipped with color televisions, telephones, and furniture which helps parents stay comfortable with their children in the hospital.

The Children's Hospital has earned a permanent place in the medical community through its truly excellent service to children and through its association with the Eastern Virginia Medical School's Graduate School of Medicine. Through a cooperative program, the pediatric specialists of tomorrow receive training from the foremost pediatric specialists of today.

All proceeds from the sale of *Dining In–Hampton Roads* will go to benefit Children's Hospital of the King's Daughters.

CONTENTS

FOREWORD

Over the past several years, we have seen our beloved Hampton Roads undergo dramatic changes. It is now the 30th largest SMSA (Standard Metropolitan Statistical Area) in the United States and is the largest between Washington, D.C. and Atlanta!

We have watched Williamsburg retain its historical character and earn a reputation as a world-class resort. We have seen the beaches of Norfolk and Virginia Beach attract over two million visitors annually. We have marveled at the exciting rebirth of the waterfronts in Norfolk and Portsmouth.

We continue to believe that the area's museums, theater, and music are among the best. The Mariners' Museum in Newport News and the Chrysler Museum in Norfolk are outstanding. The Virginia Opera Association has received national acclaim, and the Virginia Orchestra Group continues to play to "sell out" crowds. The Virginia Stage Company and other theater groups are prospering, and the new Virginia Museum of Marine Science in Virginia Beach is something we eagerly await. The Lafeyette Zoological Park in Norfolk is on the threshold of an exciting period of development.

As we have watched our region mature into a great place to live and work, we have been pleased to see the restaurants of the area help set the pace by offering a broad selection of fine fare. People naturally think of the Hampton Roads area, with its great rivers, the port, Chesapeake Bay, and the Atlantic Ocean, as a great source of seafood. We have traveled throughout the world, and we believe that not only do we have some of the most outstanding seafood restaurants to be found but that many other types of food of equal excellence are featured locally.

Through this book, we are delighted to welcome you to our home town. We invite you to visit with us, to enjoy our many great restaurants, and, as so many visitors do, to make your home in the Hampton Roads area.

Bill and Janie Whitehurst

BLUE PETE'S

Dinner for Six

Sweet Potato Biscuits

Oysters Kilpatrick

Spinach Salad

Fried Shrimp with Baked Potato and Coleslaw

Chocolate Mocha Cream Cake

Wine:

Chantfleur

Pat Ricks, Proprietor and Chef

BLUE PETE'S

In 1973, Pat Ricks, a Virginia Beach school teacher and coach, opened Blue Pete's. It was a small fishing shanty in the Pungo borough of rural Virginia Beach, with seats for about twenty people. It consisted of a beer bar, country music, pool tables, sandwiches, steamed shrimp, duck hunters, and a great deal of local color.

Gradually, the sandwich menu at Blue Pete's was replaced by fresh seafood dishes which Pat enjoyed preparing himself. The sweet potato biscuits, which have brought a great deal of recognition to the restaurant, were made from an old family recipe perfected by Pat's mother. Much of the seafood came from the *Red Fin* charter fishing boats owned by his father.

At that time, the restaurant's reputation was advertised only by word of mouth. Kathy and Bill McCarthy, food editors of *Metro Magazine*, discovered Blue Pete's in 1975. Their fantastic review brought new customers locally as well as regionally. Blue Pete's was no longer a local secret. Magazines such as *Holiday* gave the restaurant rave reviews. *Ford Times* chose Blue Pete's as "one of the best restaurants in America" and featured the sweet potato biscuits in their recipe book. The biscuit recipe, was well as many seafood dish recipes, have appeared in *Bon Appétit, Gourmet,* and the *Los Angeles Times.*

Through much hard work, Blue Pete's has grown and prospered. The same homey, casual atmosphere prevails. Pat and his wife, Betty Ann, still supervise the restaurant and greet each guest. The menu features forty seafood entrées, plus as many as a dozen varieties of fish brought in daily. The waitresses dress in colonial attire. Guests are served in one of the four inside dining rooms or on one of the two outside canopied areas overlooking Muddy Creek. Before or after dinner, guests are invited to stroll on the docks and bridges or to sit under the gazebo. The outside bar and lounge offers a scenic view where one can sit and watch customers arriving by boat. It's the perfect place to savor one of the many homemade desserts or perhaps a famous Pungo Possum.

Since 1973, Blue Pete's has grown to a 250-seat restaurant. This has not changed the fine service and the quality of food. The guest books are now filled with extremely generous compliments made by people from all over the world.

1400 North Muddy Creek Road   426-2005
Virginia Beach

SWEET POTATO BISCUITS

½ cup mashed sweet potatoes	3½-4 cups flour
½ cup sugar	1 teaspoon salt
½ cup butter	4½ teaspoons baking powder
2 tablespoons milk	1 tablespoon cinnamon

1. Mix together the sweet potatoes, sugar, butter, and milk in a large bowl.
2. Combine the flour, salt, baking powder, and cinnamon. Blend in with the first mixture. Knead until the mixture doesn't stick to the fingers.
3. Roll out the dough on a floured counter, to about ½-inch in thickness. Cut out the biscuits and place on a greased cookie sheet. Bake in a 400° oven, on the middle rack, for 14 minutes.

This famous recipe, so often requested, makes 18 fabulous biscuits.

OYSTERS KILPATRICK

36 oysters in the shell	1 bottle Worchestershire sauce
18 bacon slices	½ cup melted butter
1 tablespoon chopped parsley	1 cup grated cheddar cheese

1. Wash and shuck the oysters.
2. Place each oyster on a half shell. Crumble the cooked bacon on the oysters. Add the chopped parsley and a dash of Worchestershire. Cover each with butter and cheese.
3. Bake in a 400° oven until the oysters curl around the edge, or until the cheese melts.

Oysters Kilpatrick can be prepared 1 day ahead and refrigerated until ready to bake.

SPINACH SALAD

1 pound spinach	2 lemons
6 bacon slices, chopped	2 tablespoons honey
1 clove garlic	1 tablespoon brown sugar
¼ cup water	2 hard boiled eggs

1. Wash the spinach leaves and remove the stems.
2. Cook the chopped bacon and add a mashed clove of garlic. Sauté, then remove the clove. Add the water, juice from the lemons, honey, and brown sugar. Sauté for 5 minutes. Keep warm until ready to serve.
3. Place the prepared spinach leaves on plates. Crumble the eggs on top. Cover with hot dressing. Serve immediately.

This recipe can be prepared in advance and stored in the refrigerator. Be sure to heat the dressing before serving.

FRIED SHRIMP

2¼ pounds (10-15 count) headless shrimp	2 tablespoons Old Bay seasoning
4 eggs	2 pounds self-rising flour
1 quart milk	1 teaspoon salt
	1 teaspoon pepper

1. Peel the shrimp, leaving tails intact. Split the backside (about half the thickness) from the tail to the top. Remove the vein. Set the shrimp aside. This can be done in advance.
2. In a large bowl, beat the eggs and stir in the milk and 1 tablespoon of Old Bay.
3. In another large bowl, blend together the flour, 1 tablespoon Old Bay, salt, and pepper.

4. Take the shrimp, one at a time, and press firmly on the split, so as to flatten them only a little. Press the shrimp into the flour on both sides. Dip each one into the milk mixture and back into the flour.

5. Fry the shrimp in a deep fat fryer at 375° for 2½ minutes or until golden brown. The grease must be fresh. If you do not have a fat fryer, the shrimp can be fried in a pan and turned over, but the grease will have to be changed for better results. Serve immediately.

Always undercook seafood because it will continue to cook after it is removed from the heat. Remember—cook to color not time. Golden-colored shrimp are done to perfection.

BAKED POTATO

Wash and grease 6 potatoes with butter. Sprinkle tops with popcorn salt. Bake on the bottom rack of the oven at 425° for 45 minutes.

MARINATED COLESLAW

1 head cabbage	½ cup sugar
1 green pepper	¼ tablespoon dry mustard
1 medium onion	1 tablespoon celery seed
1 medium carrot	¼ cup vegetable oil
1 cup white vinegar	1 teaspoon salt
	1 pinch pepper

1. Chop the cabbage, dice the green pepper, slice the onion, and grate the carrot. Place all the vegetables in a bowl. Do not mix.

2. Boil the vinegar, sugar, mustard, celery seed, oil, salt, and pepper for 2 minutes.

3. Pour the boiling liquid over the vegetables. Cover and put in the refrigerator for a least 4 hours.

This cole slaw can be prepared up to two weeks in advance and stored in the refrigerator.

CHOCOLATE MOCHA CREAM CAKE

3 ounces baking chocolate	1 teaspoon baking soda
1½ cups water	½ teaspoon salt
¾ cup butter	MOCHA CREAM
2¼ cups brown sugar	ICING
2 eggs	Whipped cream
1 teaspoon vanilla	Strawberries
2¼ cups unsifted cake flour	

1. Break the chocolate into pieces; place in a small saucepan with ½ cup water and cook over low heat, stirring constantly, until the chocolate has melted. Set aside to cool.
2. Cream the butter and sugar in a large bowl until light and fluffy. Add the eggs and vanilla. Beat well. Blend in the chocolate.
3. Combine the flour, baking soda, and salt. Add the flour mixture alternately, with the remaining 1 cup of water, to the egg mixture, with mixer on low speed.
4. Pour the batter into two 8 or 9-inch greased, floured pans. Bake at 350° for 30-35 minutes. Cool for 10 minutes and remove from the pans.
5. After the cake has cooled, spread Mocha Cream on the tops. Form two layers. Chill for 1 hour. Cut into 6 equal rectangular pieces.
6. Dip each cake piece into the prepared Icing. Refrigerate until 15 minutes before serving. Garnish with whipped cream and strawberries.

MOCHA CREAM

1 ounce baking chocolate	1 cup whipping cream
1 teaspoon water	½ cup confectioners sugar
	1 teaspoon instant coffee

1. Melt the chocolate with water in a saucepan on low heat.
2. Whip the cream until stiff. Blend in the sugar, coffee, and cooled chocolate.

BLUE PETE'S

ICING

1 pound semi-sweet
  chocolate

¼ cup butter
⅓ cup water

Melt the chocolate and butter in a double boiler, stirring occasionally.
Add the water slowly until the mixture becomes creamy. Cool for 2
minutes.

*Serve very small portions of this dessert. It is very sweet, very rich, and very
delicious.*

CAFE LA ROUSSE

THE RED HEADS

Dinner for Six

Smithfield Ham Mousse with Spiced Pickled Figs

Consommé Bellevue with Pimiento Cream

Southside Chicken and Oysters

Almond Risotto with Winter Vegetables

Sally Lunn with Butter Balls

*Salad of Spinach, Mandarin Oranges and Purple Onions
with Sesame-Soy Dressing*

Celibacy Pie

Wines:

With Ham Mousse—Rapidan Dry Reisling, 1982

With Chicken and Oysters—Sabastiani Barbera, 1976

After Dinner—Napa Valley Chandon

Frances Price, Proprietor and Chef

Ann Hoffman, food editor of the *Virginian Pilot*, says of Cafe La Rousse: "A meal at the Red Head's Cafe is both modern and historical, as owner/chef Price improvises on recipes taken from antique cookbooks—Thomas Jefferson—and contempory texts—Julia Child. While her methods are those of the new American chefs such as Alice Waters, her goals are those of pioneers Fannie Farmer and Erma Rombauer. 'Women are the unsung heros of the hearth' says Price. 'Men are the showoffs who feel impelled to reinvent the meal.'"

The cafe menu reflects Price's Georgia roots and twenty years of travels as a food writer, editor, and publicist. It is eclectic, regional, original, familiar—with Poached Salmon, She-crab Soup, Rack of Lamb Dijonnaise, Georgia Country Captain, Chicken-Clam-Corn Pie, Sally Lunn, Brunswick Stew, Lemon and Chocolate Chess Pies, Vacherins and chocolate cakes.

The basis for her menu planning is availability in the marketplace. "We want the freshest and the best we can get, but we also work with leftovers," Price notes. "If I have lump crabmeat left from the night before, we'll have she-crab soup. It's a combination of market and frugality—and what's popular. That's the advantage with a flexible menu. We know immediately what people like and don't like."

The French-English name was chosen by Joan, the youngest of her four red-haired daughters, and reflects a French care and attitude toward cooking, rather than a French menu. Dinner is served every evening with six to eight specials that change nightly. Always included are a pasta dish, a seafood, steak, and chicken pie. The dessert menu of eight to ten items changes weekly. Soups, sandwiches, and salad platters with homemade breads and relishes are served continually.

339 West 21st Street 627-6466
Norfolk

SMITHFIELD HAM MOUSSE WITH SPICED PICKLED FIGS

1 envelope unflavored gelatin
¼ cup cold water
1 (7-ounce) jar Amber Brand
   Smithfield Ham Spread
¼ cup Durkee's Famous Sauce
½ cup mayonnaise

¼ cup dry Madeira
1 teaspoon grated shallot
1 tablespoon finely chopped
   parsley
1 cup heavy cream, whipped
   spiced pickled figs,
      for garnish

1. Soften the gelatin in water; heat to dissolve in a saucepan over medium heat.
2. Whisk in the ham spread, Durkee's Sauce, mayonnaise, wine, shallot, and parsley. Carefully fold in the whipped cream.
3. Refrigerate, covered, for several hours or overnight before service.
4. Serve with spiced pickled figs.

The mousse may be "set" in an oiled, 1-quart mold for buffet service.

Left-over ham can be puréed in a food processor and used instead of the commercial spread.

CONSOMMÉ BELLEVUE WITH PIMIENTO CREAM

Chicken stock
Clam juice, bottled

PIMIENTO CREAM

Heat together equal parts well-seasoned chicken stock and bottled clam juice. Pour into consommé cups and top with Pimiento Cream.

PIMIENTO CREAM

2 ounces drained pimientos,
   finely diced

1 cup heavy cream, whipped
   Salt, to taste

Fold the diced pimientos into the whipped cream. Season to taste with salt.

This is an American classic recipe which was popular around the turn of the century. We recently served it to the Ambassador to Luxembourg.

SOUTHSIDE CHICKEN and OYSTERS

1 quart dry white wine
1 medium yellow onion,
   coarsely chopped
1 carrot, coarsely chopped
1 stalk celery, coarsely
   chopped
½ teaspoon thyme
6 whole peppercorns
2 bay leaves

6 chicken breasts,
   boned and skinned
2 cups heavy cream
1 quart select oysters
  Flour
2 eggs, lightly beaten
  Fresh bread crumbs
  Clarified butter

1. In a 2-quart saucepan, combine the wine with the chopped vegetables and seasonings. Bring to a simmer and cook 10 minutes.
2. Strain off the liquid into a second pan and set aside. Place the chicken breasts in the pan and poach for about 10 minutes, or until barely done. Remove the chicken to a heated platter and keep warm.
3. Meanwhile, reduce the wine mixture over high heat until only 1 cup remains.
4. Add the cream and reduce heat to low. Cook, stirring frequently, until the cream is reduced by half and the sauce is thickened.
5. Return the chicken to the sauce and hold over very low heat, covered, while you sauté the oysters.
6. Drain the oysters, reserving the liquid for another use. Dip the oysters in flour, then beaten eggs, then roll in bread crumbs. Place in a single layer on a wax paper-lined pan. Refrigerate, covered, up to 4 hours.
7. About 10 minutes before service, fill a 10-inch skillet with clarified butter to a depth of ⅛ inch. When the butter is "rippling," add the oysters and sauté until golden brown, about 2 minutes per side. Add butter as necessary until all oysters are sautéed.
8. Assembly: On each dinner plate, place a chicken breast napped in cream-wine sauce and arrange 4-6 oysters around. Or heap all the chicken breasts on a heated platter, cover with sauce, and surround with the oysters.

This is Fran Price's original recipe. The chicken and the oysters are a wonderful combination in texture and flavor.

ALMOND RISSOTO WITH WINTER VEGETABLES

¼ cup butter, melted
½ cup chopped yellow onions
2 cups brown rice

5 cups chicken stock
Salt and white pepper
½ cup toasted sliced almonds
WINTER VEGETABLES

1. In melted butter, sauté the onion until tender but not browned. Stir in the rice, then the chicken stock.
2. Bring to a boil; reduce heat and cook, stirring frequently, until all liquid is absorbed and the rice is tender.
3. Season to taste with salt and white pepper. Stir in the almonds and serve with Winter Vegetables.

WINTER VEGETABLES

Caulifloweretts
Carrot slices

Broccoli buds
Butter

Blanch each vegetable separately and drain. Then combine and drench with butter.

SALLY LUNN WITH BUTTER BALLS

½ cup butter
1 cup milk
⅓ cup sugar
1 package dry yeast

3 eggs
4 cups sifted all-purpose flour
1 teaspoon salt
Butter balls

1. Melt the butter in a saucepan, add the milk, and heat until lukewarm. Remove from the heat.
2. Add the sugar and yeast. Stir until the sugar is dissolved.
3. Transfer to a mixer bowl and beat in the eggs on low speed.
4. Gradually add the flour and salt. Increase the speed and beat for 10 minutes.
5. Cover with a damp towel and proof until doubled in size.
6. Return to the mixer and beat for 5 minutes on medium speed.
7. Pour into a greased 10-inch tube pan or Turk's-head mold, let rise again until double, then bake in a preheated 350° oven for 45-50 minutes or until well-browned.
8. Serve with butter that has been formed into small balls.

Leftover Sally Lunn can be frozen and is wonderful toasted for breakfast.

CAFE LA ROUSSE

SALAD OF SPINACH, MANDARIN ORANGES AND PURPLE ONIONS WITH SESAME-SOY DRESSING

1 pound spinach
1 (8-ounce) can mandarin
   orange sections, drained

1 purple onion, sliced into
   thin rings

1. Wash the spinach leaves, dry, and tear into bite-size pieces.
2. Place the spinach on six chilled salad plates. Top with mandarin orange sections and purple onion rings.

SESAME-SOY DRESSING

⅓ cup tahini paste
⅓ cup soy sauce
⅓ cup dry sherry

⅓ cup sherry vinegar,
   or white vinegar
2 tablespoons sugar
2 cups salad oil

1. In a blender, combine the tahini, soy sauce, sherry, vinegar, and sugar.
2. Cover and blend 1 minute on high speed. Then slowly pour in the oil while the blender is on medium speed.
3. Ladle about 1½ ounces over each salad.

This is a delicious combination and a colorful presentation.

CAFE LA ROUSSE

CELIBACY PIE

COCONUT CRUST:
- 1 (7-ounce) package flaked coconut
- 4 graham crackers, finely crushed
- 2 tablespoons sugar
- ¼ cup butter, melted

CHOCOLATE COCONUT SAUCE:
- 2 ounces semi-sweet chocolate
- 1 tablespoon butter
- ½ cup canned coconut cream

FRANGELICA CHIFFON FILLING:
- 1 envelope unflavored gelatin
- ¼ cup cold water
- 4 egg yolks
- 1 cup milk
- ⅓ cup sugar
- ¼ teaspoon salt
- ⅓ cup Frangelica liqueur
- 3 egg whites

COCONUT CRUST:
Lightly mix all Crust ingredients until well blended. Press firmly into a 9-inch pie pan and bake at 350° for 10 minutes, or until golden brown. Cool.

FRANGELICA CHIFFON FILLING:
1. Soften the gelatin in water.
2. Make a custard of the yolks, milk, sugar, and salt. Cook over boiling water, whisking constantly, until the mixture will coat a metal spoon. Take off the heat and stir in the softened gelatin until dissolved. Stir in the liqueur and place in an ice bath. Whisk occasionally until the mixture mounds and will hold its shape.
3. Beat the egg whites until very stiff and dry. Beat into the custard about ⅓ of the whites, then carefully fold in the remaining whites. Spoon into the Coconut Crust and chill several hours or overnight.

CHOCOLATE COCONUT SAUCE:
Melt the chocolate with the butter over hot water. Whisk in the coconut cream. Drizzle over the chilled Chiffon Filling.

Celibacy Pie is so named because the consumption of a slice of this pie makes sex unnecessary!

La Caravelle

Dinner for Four

Kir Royale

Vietnamese Imperial Rolls

Crab and Asparagus Soup

Le Tournedos Caravelle

Crêpes Suzette

Cafe Parisian

Wines:

Macon Blanc Vintage 1981

St. Emilion

Tam Nguyen, Proprietor and Chef

LA CARAVELLE

The war in Vietnam forced millions of people to leave their homes and professions, but still worse, to leave their native land. Unlike most immigrants, the Vietnamese did not choose to come to America. It was the only chance for survival. Their survival is a tribute to their ingenuity and courage. It has also given us a chance to meet some culinary artists from the Far East and to sample some of the most delicate food in the world.

Craig Claiborne, an eminent food critic for the *New York Times*, hails the Vietnamese kitchen as "among the most outstanding on Earth."

La Caravelle is owned and operated by a Vietnamese couple, former Parisian restaurateurs, and since 1977, it has offered the perfect melding of the best cuisine of Paris and the Far East. Its quality food is presented at moderate prices amidst elegance, where one may obtain lunch and dinner, seafood, steak, or fowl. Each dish is prepared from authentic recipes and served to order with tantalizing hors d'oeuvres, delicious soups, salads, or fine wines.

The presentation of food is important to La Caravelle where the eye is treated not only to beautiful, verdant, and blossoming surroundings, but also to beautifully prepared and garnished dishes that emerge from the kitchen. La Caravelle now is a gathering spot for many food connoisseurs in Hampton Roads.

1040 Laskin Road   428-2477
Virginia Beach

KIR ROYALE

2 ounces Crème de Cassis   1 bottle champagne Brut

1. Pour ½ ounce of Crème de Cassis in each of four champagne glasses.
2. Fill each glass with champagne.

This is a simple and effervescent way to begin an evening.

VIETNAMESE IMPERIAL ROLLS

½ pound ground pork
1 medium onion,
     finely chopped
¼ pound crabmeat
1 medium carrot, minced
½ pound ground shrimp

1 ounce vermicelli
1 teaspoon minced black
     mushrooms
1 egg
   Salt and ground pepper
8 sheets rice paper,
     for wrapping

1. Combine all filling ingredients in a bowl.
2. Divide mixture into eight equal portions. Wrap in rice paper, one at a time.
3. Deep fry the rolls in peanut oil until golden brown.

By themselves, these rice paper-wrapped, deep-fried rolls serve as a crispy appetizer; for a true touch of Vietnam, dip them in Vietnamese fish sauce diluted with vinegar, lemon, and garlic.

CRAB AND ASPARAGUS SOUP

8 cups chicken stock	1 can white asparagus
½ teaspoon cornstarch	1 egg, beaten
¼ pound crabmeat	Salt and freshly ground pepper, to taste

1. Bring the chicken stock to a boil and then stir in cornstarch to give the stock a little thicker consistency.
2. Add the crabmeat and the asparagus, cut into inch-long pieces, then stir in the beaten egg. Remove from the heat, season to taste, and serve immediately.

This soup is a truly special blend of ingredients. It originated in Vietnam where white asparagus can be found fresh.

LE TOURNEDOS CARAVELLE

4 (8 ounce) tournedos (fillet steak, tenderloins)	Salt and freshly ground pepper
4 teaspoons butter	½ cup Madeira wine
1 teaspoon oil	2 teaspoons brown sauce
	½ cup sliced mushrooms

1. Fry the tournedos in a heavy pan with 2 teaspoons butter and the oil for 3-4 minutes on each side (medium rare); season with salt and pepper and then keep warm in a broiler.
2. For the sauce, deglaze the pan with the wine and brown sauce. Add the remaining butter and the sliced mushrooms; reduce the sauce to half, then pour over the tournedos, and serve immediately.

Using the most tender part of the beef, this Parisian dish melts in the mouth.

CRÊPES SUZETTE

½ cup orange juice
   concentrate
½ cup water

2 teaspoons butter
6 ounces Grand Marnier
   liqueur
8 very thin crêpes

1. Put the orange juice, water, butter, and 2 ounces of Grand Marnier liqueur in a 10-inch skillet, mix thoroughly, and bring to a boil.
2. Fold the crêpes into fourths, place in the hot orange sauce, turn once, and take the crêpes out. Arrange two crêpes on each dessert plate.
3. Warm the remaining Grand Marnier liqueur, ignite, pour over the crêpes, and serve immediately.

CAFE PARISIAN

4 ounces Grand Marnier
   liqueur

Strong, dark coffee
Whipped cream

1. Pour 1 ounce of Grand Marnier liqueur in each of four coffee mugs.
2. Fill with strong, dark coffee and top with whipped cream.

70% of our menu is devoted to Parisian cooking. Because of the French occupation of Vietnam, traditional Vietnamese cooking began to incorporate the best of the French cuisine. A new style of cooking was created with a wonderful blend of flavors.

Le Charlieu

Dinner for Four

Velouté de Crabe

Paté Campagnard

Homard à l'Américaine

Salade Jessica

Soufflé au Cointreau

Wines:

With Velouté and Paté—Vouvray Monmousseau 1982

With Homard and Salade—Beaujolais Blanc Jadot 1982

With Soufflé—Barsac Rothschild 1979

Richard and Carole Tranchand, Proprietors

Mathieu Guilloux, Head Chef

Micheline Dansin, Chef

LE CHARLIEU

In 1978 Richard and Carole Tranchand realized their dream when they created Le Charlieu, a classic French restaurant in a century-old building in downtown Norfolk. For Richard, who trained in Parisian five-star restaurants, Charlieu is a family name which can be traced back over five hundred years. His great grandfather was the Duke of Charlieu, in the Burgundy area of France. It is a noble name, and Richard is very proud of it.

The secret of Le Charlieu's success is the constant attendance of the Tranchands themselves. They create the proper ambience. They insist upon freshness, quality, and perfection in preparation. Chef Mathieu Guilloux joined them shortly after they opened their doors to Tidewater. He had worked with Richard as second chef in England. Together they select appetizers, entrées, and desserts to place on the menu which changes twice yearly. Some items always remain: the onion soup, the paté, the Escalope de Veau Charlieu. These are as much a part of the restaurant as are Richard's personality and Carole's eclectic decor.

Tidewater was a problem for them at first. Many selections failed to receive acceptance, but, as palates have been exposed to Le Charlieu's consistently high quality of offerings, the new menu has begun to be anticipated with excitement as well as enthusiasm. It is interesting that one of Richard's favorite entrées, a lobster dish, was once dropped from the menu when customers expressed dismay at the unusual preparation. In recent years there has been increasing demand for this same lobster dish at special parties. It may yet find its way back to the regular menu.

Richard and Carole Tranchand came to Eastern Virginia in part because of their love of the water and the sports it offers. They have done much to add zest and interest to the life of the international community in one of the world's best coastal locations. They treat their guests with dignity and avoid the pretentiousness which ruins good meals in some restaurants. Richard and Mathieu agree that each presentation must be a work of art, born from a recipe of specific regional origin, and designed to create for guests a very particular experience. There are no substitutes and no short cuts: they would never serve a bouillabaisse, for example, which is not a real bouillabaisse. One learns quickly at Le Charlieu to like the real thing.

112 College Place   623-7202
Norfolk

VELOUTÉ DE CRABE

½ cup + 2 tablespoons butter
1 tablespoon each finely diced
    shallot, onion, carrot,
    mushroom, celery, green
    pepper, and tomato
8 ounces crabmeat, picked
1 tablespoon brandy
1 cup fish stock

2 cups shrimp stock
    (or fish stock)
2 cups milk
    Bay leaf
    Salt and pepper, to taste
    Roux (1 tablespoon butter
    and 1 tablespoon flour)
½ cup cream

1. Melt the butter in a sauté pan. Add the diced vegetables and simmer the "brunoise" in the butter for 3-4 minutes.
2. Add the picked crab and simmer for 3 minutes more. Flambé with brandy.
3. Add the fish stock, shrimp stock, milk, and seasonings. Cook for 5 minutes.
4. Lightly thicken with a "roux" (made with 1 tablespoon melted butter and 1 tablespoon flour). Add the cream.
5. Verify the seasoning and serve.

This is a very special soup from Brittany. The recipe was created by the chef of the French restaurant I owned in England.

PATÉ CAMPAGNARD

½ pound pork butt
½ pound veal
½ pound duck livers
½ pound chicken livers
½ cup chopped shallots
½ cup chopped onions
3 garlic cloves, minced
2 tablespoons sliced almonds
2 tablespoons chopped
    mushrooms
2 tablespoons chopped parsley

3 eggs
2 teaspoons salt
½ teaspoon pepper
    Pinch each of allspice,
    tarragon, and thyme
½ cup brandy
1 tablespoon port
1 tablespoon green
    peppercorns
2 bay leaves
1 pound puff pastry dough

1. Slice the pork and veal into long strips. Set aside.
2. Mix together all the remaining ingredients except the peppercorns, bay leaves, and pastry dough. Add the pork, veal, duck and chicken livers and let marinate for 24 hours.
3. The next day, mince the meat mixture thoroughly. Then blend it to a uniform texture with a whisk or spatula.
4. Add the green peppercorns.
5. Pour the paté mixture into a deep pan and lay the bay leaves on top. Cover with aluminum foil.
6. Bake in a 350° oven, in a *bain-marie*, for 2 hours or until the center is hot.
7. Press with slabs of wood and weights to flatten. Refrigerate for 12 hours.
8. Remove the aluminum foil and bay leaves from the paté.
9. Brush melted butter on the puff pastry dough. Wrap the paté in the puff pastry dough and bake at 450° until golden brown.

This is a coarse, firm French country-style paté. All patés are different, and each is a reflection of the chef's personality.

HOMARD À L'AMÉRICAINE

4 (1¼-1½ pounds) lobsters, live
½ cup olive oil
1 tablespoon butter
¾ cup finely chopped onions
¾ cup finely chopped shallots
1 tablespoon brandy
2 cups white wine
6 ripe tomatoes, chopped
1 tablespoon tomato paste

2 quarts fish stock
Saffron, to taste
Cayenne pepper, to taste
1 bouquet garni
(parsley stems, leek, and bay leaf)
3 cloves garlic, crushed
½ cup cream
Rice Pilaf

1. Cut the live lobsters into large chunks. Reserve the creamy parts and remove the sand pouches.
2. Sauté the lobster in olive oil and butter, adding the chopped onions and then the shallots. Flambé with brandy.
3. Add the white wine, chopped tomatoes, tomato paste, fish stock, seasonings, and garlic. Bring to a boil.
4. Transfer the lobster and sauce to a 400° oven and bake for 18-20 minutes.
5. Remove the lobster from the sauce, set aside, but keep warm.
6. Reduce the sauce by half and then remove from the heat. Strain the sauce and then add to it the reserved creamy parts of the lobster. Whisk the sauce to thicken.
7. Whisk the cream into the sauce, verify the seasoning, and pour the sauce over the lobster.
8. Serve with Rice Pilaf.

This is a nasty recipe, but one of the best. You must hold the live lobster by the head and cut from the tail to the head. It must be served in the shell. The meat adheres to the shell, and to remove it would be to take the character away from the experience of eating this dish.

LE CHARLIEU

SALADE JESSICA

¼ head red cabbage	1 bunch spinach
2 apples, sliced	½ cup grated carrots
3 cups red wine vinegar	½ cup chopped walnuts
1 head leaf lettuce	Vinaigrette dressing

1. Finely slice the red cabbage. Marinate the cabbage and the apples in the vinegar for 12 hours.
2. When ready to serve, tear the lettuce and spinach into bite-size pieces. For each serving, place half lettuce and half spinach on the salad plate. Top with marinated cabbage and decorate with apple slices, 2 tablespoons grated carrots, and 2 tablespoons walnuts.
3. Serve with vinaigrette dressing.

The tartness of this salad serves to wash the palate, which is a very important thing to do between courses.

SOUFFLÈ AU COINTREAU

8 eggs
3 tablespoons flour
¼ cup sugar
1 quart milk

1 tablespoon unsalted butter
3 tablespoons Cointreau
Butter, for greasing mold
Sugar, for dusting mold

1. Separate the eggs, reserving all the egg whites and setting aside 5 egg yolks. Refrigerate the whites.
2. Mix together the 5 egg yolks, flour, and sugar.
3. Bring the milk and butter to a boil.
4. Pour the milk over the egg yolk mixture, heating to a boil while mixing. Immediately cool over ice. Add the Cointreau.
5. Coat a soufflé mold with butter and dust with sugar.
6. Beat the egg whites until firm.
7. Dilute the egg yolk mixture with 2 spoons of egg whites and then gently fold in the remaining whites.
8. Pour into the prepared mold. Bake at 425° for 25 minutes.

Cointreau is used in this dessert rather than Grand Marnier because it is not as rich or as strong. The flavor of the Cointreau blends with the flavors of this meal and with the wines selected.

THE ESPLANADE

Dinner for Six

Lobster Bisque en Croûte

Esplanade Salad with Roquefort Dressing

Veal Chanterelle

Stuffed Eggplant

Amaretto Mousse

Wines:

With Soup and Salad—Clos du Bois
Early Harvest Johannisberg Reisling, 1982

With Veal—Château St. Jean Chardonnay, Robert Young, 1980

Omni International Hotel, Proprietor

Michael Sigler, Executive Chef

THE ESPLANADE

Omni International Hotel continues to set the standard for quality and excellence. One of its best examples, The Esplanade, offers the finest in regionalized American cuisine. Artistic presentations of color boldly accent the flavor of fresh local and domestic ingredients. An abundant selection of boutique varietals creates a wine list that encompasses vintages from all over the world. Gracious service in the classical tradition enhances the warmth of the rich 38-seat parlor setting.

Exceptional young apprentices, who had trained arduously to learn the classic disciplines, joined the Omni culinary team in 1976. Their mentor, Executive Chef Michael Sigler, inspires and directs their innovative and creative talents. Special respect for ingredients has led to the most familiar statements about the cuisine: that its style is lighter and simpler, without heavy sauces; that vegetables are served crisp-tender; that seafood is cooked quickly with perfect timing; that salads and first courses are unusual but never overwhelm a meal; that desserts are delicate and light.

Omni International Hotel believes in its culinary team. Their combined talents have been internationally acclaimed. Chef Michael Sigler returned from Bad Gleichenberg, Austria, with an Olympic Culinary Gold Medal. The vitality of American ingredients and composition had been, for the first time, internationally recognized. This excitement led them to the next step in national competition. The results were two silver medals, two bronze, and a silver cup in the 1983 American Culinary Federation competition. The Esplanade remains a fine example of excellence in the preparation and presentation of a truly American cuisine.

Omni International Hotel   623-0333
On the River at Waterside
Norfolk

LOBSTER BISQUE EN CROÛTE

2 ounces butter
¼ cup flour
1 (1½-pound) lobster
1 stalk celery
1 medium onion
½ cup French brandy
1 shallot, chopped

1 quart fish stock
¼ cup white wine
Pinch of saffron
1 teaspoon tomato purée
1 cup heavy cream
1 tablespoon lobster base
Puff pastry dough
Egg wash

1. Make a *roux* with butter and flour.
2. Break the lobster up in sections. Roughly chop the celery and onion (white *mirepoix*). Brown the onions, celery, and lobster meat in a 425° oven; stir every 10-15 minutes.
3. Remove from the oven when browned and place on the range; flame with French brandy. Add the shallots, fish stock, and white wine; let simmer for at least 1 hour. Cool slightly and strain through a fine sieve.
4. To the strained bisque, add the saffron, tomato purée, cream, and lobster base to taste.
5. Thicken the bisque with the *roux* to desired consistency.
6. At time of service, fill six oven-proof serving dishes with the bisque. Egg wash the rim of each dish and top with the puff pastry dough. Egg wash the puff pastry and bake in 425° oven until golden brown and puffed.

We find this bisque to be particularly nice because of the saffron flavoring. Saffron is very complimentary to seafood, enhancing its flavor.

ESPLANADE SALAD with ROQUEFORT DRESSING

3 heads hydroponic
  Bibb lettuce
3 large hydroponic
  Beefsteak tomatoes

1 red onion
6 ounces ROQUEFORT
  DRESSING

1. Wash and separate the lettuce. Core, wash, and slice the tomatoes. Peel and wash the red onion.
2. Divide the lettuce evenly between six salad plates. Off to the side of each lettuce mound, lay one slice of tomato, one slice of onion, and finish with one slice of tomato.
3. Serve with Roquefort Dressing or another favorite dressing.

ROQUEFORT DRESSING

3 ounces Roquefort cheese,
  crumbled

1 cup mayonnaise
1 clove garlic, minced

Combine all ingredients and mix thoroughly.

We have found that hydroponic vegetables—those grown in water—are of superior quality. These vegetables retain their nutrients and taste better, too.

VEAL CHANTERELLE

1½ pounds veal loin, trimmed
 (4-ounce portions)
2 teaspoons minced shallots
½ cup brandy
6 ounces chanterelles
 (wild French mushrooms)

6 ounces cream
10 ounces DEMI-GLAZE
 Salt and pepper, to taste
4 ounces vegetables,
 julienned (sliced thin)

1. Sauté the veal loins.
2. Remove the veal from the pan and add shallots.
3. Deglaze the pan with brandy; add the chanterelles and cream; let the liquid reduce.
4. Add Demi-glaze, salt, and pepper to taste.
5. Serve veal with chanterelle sauce and garnish with julienned vegetables.

DEMI-GLAZE

1 pound veal bones
1 carrot
1 onion
2 cloves garlic

½ stalk celery
4 sprigs fresh thyme
1 bay leaf
2 cups red wine
2 gallons water

1. Roast the veal bones in a very hot oven (500°) until browned, 10-15 minutes.
2. Add the vegetables, seasonings, and red wine and remove from the oven.
3. Transfer to a large kettle and add the water. Simmer until reduced by two-thirds. Cool slightly and strain through a fine sieve.
4. If a thicker demi-glaze is desired, add *roux* (equal parts butter and flour) until of desired consistency.

Your dish is only as good as the demi-glaze. If the demi-glaze is good, the dish will be good.

STUFFED EGGPLANT

3 small eggplants
Garlic powder, to taste
¼ teaspoon freshly ground
   black pepper
1 zucchini
1 yellow squash
4 medium tomatoes
2 onions
1 green pepper

1 clove garlic, minced
2 teaspoons olive oil
¼ teaspoon oregano
1½ teaspoons salt
½ teaspoon sugar
2 tablespoons chopped
   parsley
2 tablespoons lemon juice
1 cup white wine

1. Slice the eggplants lengthwise, scoop out some of the insides, and flatten bottoms so boats (eggplants) lie flat. Season with a little garlic and ⅛ teaspoon black pepper. Steam in a steamer for 1 minute and then set aside to cool.

2. To prepare the stuffing, dice the zucchini and yellow squash. Peel, seed, and dice the tomatoes. Cut the onions and green peppers into ¼-inch slices.

3. Sauté the minced garlic in the olive oil; add the onions, green peppers, zucchini, and yellow squash. Cook over medium heat until tender. Add the tomato, oregano, ⅛ teaspoon pepper, salt, sugar, parsley, and lemon juice; add the white wine and simmer for 10 minutes. Fill the eggplant boats and bake for 10 minutes at 325°; remove and **serve** immediately.

For a delicious variation, sprinkle each filled eggplant boat with shredded Mozzarella cheese before baking.

AMARETTO MOUSSE

1 pint whipping cream
1 tablespoon gelatin powder
3 ounces Amaretto liqueur
4 eggs

3 tablespoons confectioners sugar
Vanilla extract, to taste
Almond extract, to taste
1 cup sliced, toasted almonds

1. Whip the fresh, heavy cream. Place in the refrigerator until ready to use.
2. Dissolve the gelatin powder in Amaretto in a double boiler. Keep warm until ready to use.
3. Combine the eggs and confectioners sugar in a separate double boiler. Heat on low temperature until warm while whisking constantly.
4. Remove the egg and sugar mixture from the heat and mix at high speed until consistency reaches firm peaks.
5. Fold the gelatin mixture into the eggs.
6. Fold in the whipped cream and add vanilla and almond extract to taste.
7. Fill dessert glasses and place in the refrigerator until firm (approximately 1 hour).
8. Garnish with sliced, toasted almonds.

This mousse is a very light dessert. It is a good recipe to serve after a meal of many courses.

Henry's Seafood Restaurant

Dinner for Four

Henry's "Famous" She-Crab Soup

Lettuce and Tomato Salad
House Dressing

Shrimp Stuffed with Fresh Chesapeake Bay Crabmeat

Deep-Fried Fresh "Loligo" Squid

Wine:

Mirassou—Monterey Riesling

Henry, Carol, and Anna Braithwaite, Proprietors

Johnny Young, Chef

HENRY'S SEAFOOD RESTAURANT

Henry's Seafood Restaurant was started in 1962 by Henry S. Braithwaite and his wife Anna. It started out as an oyster and clam bar that served oysters and clams on the half shell, crab-cake sandwiches, oyster stew, clam chowder, and she-crab soup. Henry sold steamed crabs, live crabs, oysters in the shell, and shucked oysters by the pint and quart.

In 1968 Henry was joined by his son Henry Jr. (known by most people as Tuffy). Since 1967 Henry's has gone through four major additions and now seats around 180 people. It has a very nice patio dining area overlooking the famous Lynnhaven River and a dock where customers may arrive by boat as well. It has a very good winter business supported by many local patrons. Summertime at Henry's is a most popular season. "Ours is a family-run business," explains Henry Braithwaite, Jr. "We pride ourselves on serving the freshest of local seafood. Our own fishing boat, the *Anna Marie*, brings us the best seafood available in the waters off the Virginia coast and in the Chesapeake Bay."

3319 Shore Drive   481-7300
Virginia Beach

HENRY'S SEAFOOD RESTAURANT

SHE-CRAB SOUP

1 quart fresh milk	2 teaspoons dry parsley flakes
½ pound real butter	⅛ teaspoon white pepper
1 teaspoon Seafood Seasoning (McCormick's)	½ teaspoon garlic powder
4 teaspoons onion salt (McCormick's)	¼ cup cornstarch
1 teaspoon garlic salt (McCormick's)	1 pound fresh Backfin crabmeat (Chesapeake Bay)
	½ bottle sweet white wine

1. Place the milk and butter in a large pot and set on the stove over medium heat. When the butter has melted (do not boil the milk), add all of the ingredients except the crabmeat, cornstarch, and wine. Add the ingredients one at a time, stirring between each.

2. When the soup base is *hot*, add the cornstarch to thicken as desired. Then add the crabmeat and stir into the base, mixing in well, making sure all the crabmeat has been separated.

3. As the soup is poured into the bowls for serving, add a *good* tablespoon of wine to each bowl!

She-Crab Soup is a regional favorite. The name describes a crab soup made with a white, milk base. He-Crab soup has a red, or tomato, base.

LETTUCE AND TOMATO SALAD
WITH HENRY'S HOUSE DRESSING

Lettuce　　　　　　　　　　*Carrots*
Tomatoes　　　　　　　　　*Other garden vegetables*
Onions　　　　　　　　　　*HENRY'S HOUSE DRESSING*

Place all ingredients in a large salad bowl and place in the refrigerator until serving time. Portion out salad into bowls and add Henry's House Dressing.

HENRY'S SEAFOOD RESTAURANT

HENRY'S HOUSE DRESSING

½ onion, diced
½ cup apple cider vinegar
   Salt, to taste
   Pepper, to taste

¼ cup sugar (or less)
½ tablespoon dry mustard
¼ cup salad oil
¼ cup water

1. Soak the onions in the vinegar for a short while.
2. Add all the remaining ingredients and mix well.
3. If the dressing is too sweet, add more vinegar.

STUFFED SHRIMP

4 large shrimp
  (16-20 count, or larger)
1 pound fresh Backfin
  crabmeat
1 egg

¼ cup Durkee's Famous Sauce
1 tablespoon mayonnaise
1 cup Italian flavored
  bread crumbs
Salt, to taste
¼ stick of butter

1. Peel and devein the shrimp, leaving the tail on and splitting down the back, reaching almost all the way through the underside.
2. In a bowl, separate the crabmeat. Add the egg, Durkee's Famous Sauce, mayonnaise, bread crumbs, and salt to taste. Mix all ingredients together well.
3. Make four balls out of ingredients, making sure they hold together.
4. Place the balls of mixed crabmeat on the split shrimp backs. Shape into a mound on each shrimp. After all the shrimp have been stuffed, sprinkle the outside of each with more Italian-flavored bread crumbs.
5. Place the shrimp in an ovenproof dish and place one ¼-inch slice of butter on each. Place the shrimp under the broiler until golden brown, basting from time to time with the melted butter from the dish.

Henry Braithwaite, Sr. created this recipe, and it is a family favorite as well as a best-selling menu item. It is served as an entrée with a baked potato and either coleslaw or a green salad.

DEEP-FRIED SQUID

2 pounds fresh "Loligo"
  squid
Milk

2 cups flour
½ tablespoon pepper
1 tablespoon garlic salt
  Oil, for frying

1. Clean and skin the squid both inside and out and cut into rings about ⅛ to ¼-inch in thickness. Place in a bowl containing enough milk to cover.
2. Mix the flour, black pepper, and garlic salt together, blending well.
3. Heat the oil in a deep-fat fryer to 350°.
4. The squid should now be taken out of the milk and coated with the flour mixture, each ring being separated from the others. Drop the squid into the fryer basket and then into hot oil for two to four minutes, depending on how many rings and the size of the rings. Fry until golden brown, then remove from the basket, and allow to drain. Serve the rings hot with favorite sauces.

Squid is becoming more and more popular as people are exposed to it. This recipe can be served as an appetizer or as a main dish.

The Iron Gate House

Dinner for Six

Camembert Frit

Mussels Provençal

Cabbage and Onion Soup au Gruyère

*Iron Gate Salad
with Champagne and Mustard Dressing*

Tenderloin of Beef Henry IV

Chocolate Espresso Cheesecake

Wines:

*With Camembert Frit—Johannisberg Riesling
Chateau St. Jean, Robert Young Vineyards 1982*

*With Mussels, Soup, and Salad—Sauvignon Blanc
Concannon 1981*

*With Tenderloin—Cabernet Sauvignon
Beaulieu Vineyard, Georges De Latour Private Reserve 1978*

*With Cheesecake—Perrier Jouët,
Fleur De Champagne 1976*

*Todd Jurich, Kirk Oliver, and Meg Williams, Proprietors
Todd Jurich and Meg Williams, Chefs*

THE IRON GATE HOUSE

The Iron Gate House, located on 36th Street and Atlantic Avenue in Virginia Beach, has been in operation since 1977. The restaurant, once a beach house, has a semi-formal, yet home-like atmosphere with a fireplace in the main dining room. Kirk Oliver, one of the owners, welcomes each guest at the door. Waiters, attired in blue blazers, greet the diners warmly and explain the menu selections for the evening. A five-course meal begins with a house appetizer and is followed by the chef's choice of a homemade soup or pasta and a fresh green salad. The diner then selects an entrée from the list of roast rack of lamb, tenderloin of beef, veal, roast duckling, or seafood. All items change every few days depending on what is fresh and seasonal. The meal is completed with the selection of an irresistible homemade dessert. Todd Jurich and Meg Williams, who are both the chefs and owners, are always happy to accommodate special orders for five-course vegetarian dinners within a day's notice.

"We strive to create a comfortable feeling for our guests," explains Todd Jurch. "We want each person to feel as if he or she is enjoying a leisurely five-course meal in a good friend's home."

36th Street at Atlantic Avenue   422-5748
Virginia Beach

THE IRON GATE HOUSE

CAMEMBERT FRIT

1 cup flour
⅓ cup cornstarch
2 teaspoons paprika
1 cold beer

Assortment of fresh fruit
3 (4½-ounce) rounds
   Camembert cheese
Cooking oil
   (at least 3" deep in pan)

1. Mix the flour, cornstarch, and paprika in a bowl. Slowly add the beer, a little at a time, to the mixture and whip with a wire whisk until it reaches the consistency of pancake batter.
2. Slice the fruits (apples, strawberries, blueberries, melon, bananas, oranges, red grapes, kiwi, etc.) and arrange on individual plates.
3. Cut each cheese round into quarters. Dip the cheese into the batter and drop into hot (350°) oil for approximately 1 minute. Remove from the oil and place (2 each) on fruit plates and serve.

The beer batter for this appetizer is very light. The combination of cheese and fruit makes this a palatable beginning to a meal.

MUSSELS PROVENÇAL

1 cup dry white wine
Juice of 1 lemon
1 cup GARLIC BUTTER
9-12 mussels per serving

1 pound fresh egg linguini
  or fetuccine
1 cup grated fresh
  Parmesan cheese
Lemon wedges

1. Place the white wine in a saucepan along with the lemon juice and Garlic Butter. Bring to boil, add the mussels, and steam until opened, about 5 minutes.
2. Arrange mussels on a bed of pasta (cooked *al dente*), ladle juice over the mussels, and finish by generously dusting with Parmesan cheese. Serve immediately with lemon wedges.

GARLIC BUTTER

1 pound unsalted butter,
  softened
1 tablespoon freshly chopped
  parsley (pressed)
2 tablespoons white wine
1 tablespoon Pernod

1 tablespoon brandy
½ tablespoon garlic salt
1 tablespoon finely minced
  fresh garlic
1 tablespoon finely minced
  fresh shallots

Combine all ingredients in a bowl or blender.

This is a very versatile recipe: it is a delicious second course but also makes a delightful main course.

CABBAGE AND ONION SOUP AU GRUYÈRE

3 quarts favorite beef stock
   (preferably homemade)
1 head green cabbage,
   jullienned
1 teaspoon celery seed

3 medium yellow onions,
   jullienned
2 pinches nutmeg
¼ cup cream sherry
1 cup grated Gruyère cheese

1. Pour the beef stock into a large stockpan and add all of the ingredients except the sherry and Gruyère. Simmer 1½ hours or until all the vegetables are cooked.
2. Remove from the heat, still keeping very warm but being careful not to burn.
3. Just before serving, add sherry to taste. Place cheese in the bottom of each bowl and ladle in the soup. Serve immediately.

This soup keeps for up to one week in the refrigerator and is even better when reheated.

IRON GATE SALAD
WITH CHAMPAGNE AND MUSTARD DRESSING

1 head leaf lettuce	CHAMPAGNE AND
1 head red leaf lettuce	MUSTARD DRESSING
12 cherry tomatoes, halved	6 tablespoons bacon bits
6 raw mushrooms, sliced	6 tablespoons toasted almonds

1. Wash, dry, and prepare the vegetables for the salad.
2. Arrange the lettuce leaves on the salad plates. Top with the cherry tomatoes and mushroom slices.
3. Spoon dressing over the greens and then sprinkle 1 tablespoon bacon bits and 1 tablespoon toasted almonds over the top of each salad.

CHAMPAGNE AND MUSTARD DRESSING

½ cup Dijon mustard	¼ cup red wine vinegar
10 egg yolks	¾ cup champagne
2 pinches of freshly ground (coarse) pepper	2 teaspoons chicken stock
	2¼ cups cotton seed oil

Combine all of the ingredients except the cotton seed oil in a food processor. Blend well adding oil slowly until of desired thickness, adjust to taste, and refrigerate 1 hour or longer.

We vary the vegetables in this salad depending on what is the best available in the market. A mixture of greens is also a nice change.

TENDERLOIN OF BEEF HENRY IV

6 *tenderloins of beef*	*BORDELAISE SAUCE*
Butter	*BÉARNAISE SAUCE*
6 *large, round croutons*	6 *large artichoke bottoms*
(same size as tenderloin)	

1. Sauté the tenderloin fillets in a skillet with butter to desired doneness (medium rare or rare preferably). Set aside on a platter while preparing Bordelaise and Béarnaise Sauces.

2. To assemble dish for serving, place a round crouton about the same size as the fillet on a warm serving platter. Place a heated fillet on top of each crouton, followed with Bordelaise Sauce. Sauté the artichoke bottoms which are then placed on top. Finnish off with the Béarnaise covering.

BORDELAISE SAUCE

½ *cup chopped shallots*	*Sprig of thyme*
2 *tablespoons unsalted butter*	*(wild or cultivated)*
¼ *cup dry brandy*	1 *cup basic brown sauce*
2 *cups good dry red wine*	2 *ounces fresh beef marrow*
(Red Bordeaux)	*Butter, to thicken*
Small bay leaf	

1. In the skillet used to cook the beef, sauté the shallots in the unsalted butter until lightly browned and then flame with brandy.

2. Add the wine and spices and bring to a boil until reduced by half. Add the brown sauce and boil 20 minutes, skimming off impurities.

3. Poach the marrow in salted water for 5 minutes, drain, and add to the sauce. When ready to serve, heat in skillet and add whole butter to thicken.

continued...

BÉARNAISE SAUCE

¼ cup white wine
1 teaspoon finely chopped
   shallots
2 tablespoons cream sherry
6 egg yolks
   Juice of ½ lemon
2 dashes of white pepper

1 good dash of Tabasco
½ teaspoon Worcestershire
½ teaspoon Dijon mustard
¾ cup clarified butter, warm
1 tablespoon chopped fresh
   tarragon leaves

1. In a saucepan combine the white wine, shallots, and sherry and boil until reduced by half. Set aside.

2. In a food processor, place all remaining ingredients except the butter and tarragon. Start blending and dribbling in the butter slowly and steadily until the mixture emulsifies into the thickness of a pancake batter. Follow by adding the shallot mixture until smooth. Complete the sauce by folding in tarragon leaves. Keep warm until served.

Good accompaniments for this elegant dish are Parsley New Potatoes, Sautéed Snow Peas, and Glazed Baby Belgium Carrots.

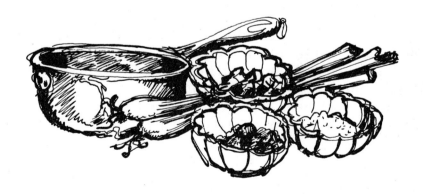

CHOCOLATE ESPRESSO CHEESECAKE

FILLING:
- 1½ pounds cream cheese
- 1¼ cups white sugar
- 1 teaspoon vanilla extract
- 6 whole eggs
- ½ cup melted semi-sweet chocolate
- 3 tablespoons Kahlua
- 1 pinch of salt
- ¼ cup freshly brewed espresso, cooled down

CRUST:
- 1 cup graham cracker crumbs
- 3 tablespoons clarified butter, melted
- ¼ cup sugar

ICING:
- 1½ cups sour cream
- ½ cup sugar
- 1 teaspoon vanilla extract

1. FILLING: Combine all of the Filling ingredients in food processor until smooth (adding cream cheese gradually).
2. CRUST: Combine dry ingredients together, then drizzle in melted butter. Press mixture into a 10-inch springform pan.
3. Pour the Filling into the Crust and bake for 1 hour and 20 minutes, or until firm.
4. ICING: Mix all ingredients together well. Set aside.
5. Remove the cheesecake from the oven, top with the Icing and bake for 10 minutes more. Refrigerate for 3 hours before serving.

You don't have to like expresso to like this cheesecake; however, a small slice goes well with a cup of expresso and a snifter of brandy.

KYOTO
JAPANESE RESTAURANT

Dinner for Six

Yaki Tori

Sashimi

Scallops

Tempura

Sunomono

Beef Teriyaki and King Crab Legs

Wine:

Sake or Plum Wine

Henry Kuwabara, Proprietor and Chef

KYOTO

Named for the ancient capital city of Japan, Kyoto, greater Hampton Roads' only authentic Japanese restaurant, offers a superb dining experience. The tatami rooms, native art, and delicate Japanese floral arrangements provide an atmosphere of serenity and hospitality.

Patrons enjoy the popular Sushi, Sukiyaki, and a wide variety of Tempuras among the many exquisitely prepared delicacies and delight in the skillful presentation of each menu selection.

Owner Henry Kuwabara has served numerous celebrities in his popular restaurant. Among the notables are Kirk Douglas, Katherine Ross, Martin Sheen, Michele Lee, and Eartha Kitt. Since 1976, local personalities of discriminating taste have enjoyed the combination of tranquil surroundings and the finest in ethnic cuisine.

432 Newtown Road   499-1657
Virginia Beach

YAKI TORI

1 *whole breast of chicken,*
cut in small cubes

2 *onions, cut in small cubes*
or triangles
Teriyaki sauce

1. Preheat a broiler or prepare a charcoal grill.
2. Alternating ingredients, thread the chicken and onions on bamboo skewers.
3. Brush with teriyaki sauce and broil the brochettes until done and tender.

Teriyaki sauce is available at Japanese grocers and Oriental markets.

A Japanese dinner is composed of courses reflecting a series of cooking techniques. The dishes prepared may vary, but the combination and order should be maintained: zensai (appetizer), soup, salad, agemono (deep-fried foods), yakimono (broiled dishes), dessert, and tea.

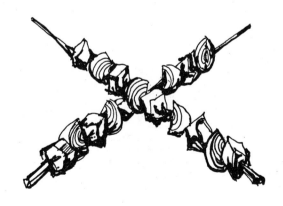

SASHIMI

24 slices raw flounder
(4 per person)

Hot mustard
Soy sauce

1. Roll the flounder slices into the shape of a rose petal.
2. Serve with hot mustard.
3. Stir a drop of mustard in soy sauce; dip sashimi in sauce to eat.

SCALLOPS

24 medium-size pieces of
scallops (4 per person)

Salt and pepper
Flour

1. Sprinkle scallops with salt and pepper.
2. Shake in flour.
3. Grease a sauté pan (just enough to wet the surface).
4. Cook over low heat for 30-40 minutes, turning occasionally, until crisp.

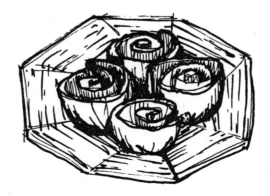

TEMPURA

12 raw shrimp or prawns
 6 raw scallops
 ½ pound fish fillets,
     cut in 1½"x2" pieces
 1 green pepper, cut in
     1½"x2" pieces
 1 sweet potato, peeled
     or 3 carrots, peeled and
     cut diagonally in ¼" slices

 ¼ pound green beans or
     asparagus tips, cut in
     bite-size pieces
    Vegetable oil
 3 cups sifted cake flour
 1 tablespoon baking powder
 2 egg yolks
    TEMPURA SAUCE

1. Clean and butterfly the shrimp, leaving the tails intact. Cut the scallops in half if they are too large. Set aside.
2. Drain the seafood and vegetables thoroughly on paper towels. Arrange on a large platter.
3. Pour the oil at least 2 inches deep in an electric fry pan or deep, wide fry pan. Heat the oil to 350°. If you don't have a thermometer, test the oil by dropping a piece of vegetable into the pan. It should float.
4. Sift the flour and baking powder together. Set aside. Thoroughly beat the egg yolks with a wire whisk or hand beater and stir in the flour quickly until it is moistened and the large lumps disappear. The batter should be very lumpy and the consistency of whipping cream. Do not stir the batter after it is mixed.
5. Coat the ingredients with the batter, starting with the shrimp. Slightly drain off the excess batter and slide into the hot oil. Fry about 1 minute. Turn over and fry 1 minute longer or until cooked to a light golden brown; remove. Dip and fry the other ingredients in the same manner. Skim off bits of cooked batter. Drain on paper towels or a wire rack.
6. Line a small bowl with a paper towel or an open basket with paper. In it, place an assortment of tempura along with a container of the Tempura Sauce. Dip each piece in the sauce before eating.

The color of tempura comes from the oil rather than the batter. The secret of good color is in using a blend of new and used oil. Never cook too much food at once or the oil temperature will drop. The oil temperature should be 335°-350°. The tempura should never be soggy. Hot or cold, the batter should be crisp.

TEMPURA SAUCE

4 cups dashi   2 teaspoons sugar
¼ cup Japanese shoyu sauce

Combine all ingredients in a saucepan. Heat until warm.

*Japanese shoyu sauce must be used when making this sauce. The American
variety adds a different flavor to the dish. Or you might substitute Kikkoman
tempura sauce and follow directions on the label. Instant dashi, a variation
of the soup stock made from dried bonito shavings, is available at Japanese
markets.*

SUNOMONO

1½ pounds cucumbers,   ½ cup sugar
      peeled and thinly sliced   Cooked crab
      Salt   Cooked shrimp
¾ cup cider vinegar   Tomato slices

1. Sprinkle the cucumbers lightly with salt. Allow to stand at room
   temperature for 1 hour.
2. Thoroughly blend together ¾ teaspoon salt, the vinegar, and sugar.
   Stir until the sugar dissolves.
3. Add ¼ cup of this vinegar sauce to the cucumbers. Stir lightly and
   drain. Just before serving, pour the remaining sauce over the cucumbers. Serve in individual bowls and garnish with cooked crab,
   shrimp, and tomato slices.

BEEF TERIYAKI

6 *(5-ounce) Delmonico steaks*   *Teriyaki sauce, bottled*

1. Broil the steaks to medium rare.
2. Slice the steaks about ¼-inch thick. Brush teriyaki sauce over the steak slices and serve hot.

KING CRAB LEGS

12 *pieces King Crab legs,*   ½ *cube butter, melted*
   cut 3"-4" each

1. Heat the crab legs under the broiler until hot.
2. Pour melted butter over the legs and serve hot.

LE YACA

Dinner for Four

Crouton des Mers du Nord

Petite Bourride à ma Facon

Chiffonnade de Scarole

Fillet de Boeuf à la Ficelle
Entouré de ses Légumes—Sauce Béarnaise

Brie de Meaux et Vieux Chaumes

La Marquise au Chocolat du ya ca

Wines:

Puilly Fumé, Nicolas 1982

Chateau Kirwan, Margaux 1977

Danièle Bourderau, Proprietor and Chef

LE YA CA

Le ya ca, Restaurant Francais, first opened in 1964 in an old pleasant farm house near a mountain ski resort in France. Though Courchevel was eight kilometers of icy road away, the restaurant became a favorite almost immediately. The huge fireplace in the middle of the dining room, with the legs of lamb hanging in front of the fire, remains the main attraction of the customers.

The second *Le ya ca* restaurant has been open for some time in St. Tropez in the South of France on the Mediterranean Sea, keeping the same formula. A barbecue has been built in the garden, and legs of lamb are cooked in front of it.

In 1980 *Le ya ca*, Williamsburg, was opened. After looking in other states, Williamsburg, Virginia, was chosen for its European flair, and the restaurant itself has the feeling of a French country estate. Each table is magnificently set with antique lace cloths, crystal, and china.

The owner of the Williamsburg *Le ya ca* is Danièle Bourderau, a native Frenchwoman, who oversees every element of the restaurant's operation. She personally greets the diners at the table and explains the entrées and their preparation. She explains how the restaurant got its name when she tells about opening her first restaurant in the farmhouse in France. "People told us we were crazy, that we would never make it. So we named it *Le ya ca*, which is a contraction meaning *Let's* because on the day we decided to go ahead with the project we just said, 'Let's do it, and we'll see what happens!'"

1915 Pocahontas Trail   220-3616
Williamsburg

LE YA CA

CROUTON DES MERS DU NORD

4 (1½"x1½") croutons,
   French bread, or toast
3 scrambled eggs

1 teaspoon finely chopped
   spring onion
2 ounces smoked salmon,
   thinly sliced

On each crouton, place a portion of scrambled egg mixed with chopped spring onion, then top with small strips of smoked salmon, cut the same width and shape as the crouton.

This appetizer is very light and easy to eat. It's a pleasant way to start the meal. I've never met anyone who didn't like it.

PETITE BOURRIDE À MA FACON

⅜ cup olive oil
1 medium onion, peeled
   and finely chopped
1 medium leek, white part
   only, chopped
1 large clove of garlic,
   peeled and finely chopped
2 medium tomatoes, peeled
   seeded, and chopped

1½ pound monk fish or rockfish
1 generous pinch of saffron
   Pepper and salt, to taste
   Bouquet garni
4 cups water
⅜ cup dry white wine
1 pound shrimp (35-40 count)
   AIOLI SAUCE
   Parsley

1. In a large pot, heat the olive oil, then add the chopped onion, leek, and garlic. Sauté the vegetables over low heat, uncovered, for 15 minutes, stirring occasionally to keep them from sticking or coloring. Add the chopped tomatoes and continue cooking, uncovered, for an additional 5 minutes.
2. Lay the fish on top of vegetables, season with saffron and a little pepper and salt to taste. Then add the bouquet garni, water, and wine.
3. Place on high heat and cook to a rapid boil, uncovered, until the fish is nearly cooked, then add the shrimp and let boil for an additional 2 minutes. Set aside.
4. Prepare the Aioli Sauce as the fish cools slightly.
5. After the sauce is finished, peel the shrimp. Take out the white fillet of fish. Strain the bouillon. Let it reduce a little, then mix the sauce in whisking constantly with the bouillon. Be careful the bouillon does not boil when adding the Aioli Sauce. Serve in separate deep dishes, each with 3 shrimp and a fillet of fish covered with the bouillon. Sprinkle a little parsley on top.

LE YA CA

AIOLI SAUCE

2 egg yolks
   Salt and pepper, to taste
1 clove garlic, peeled and
   finely chopped

1 teaspoon Dijon mustard
1 pint olive oil
1 teaspoon lemon juice
1 dash of Tabasco or
   Texas Pete

1. Place the yolks, salt, pepper, garlic, and mustard in bowl. Beat together with a whisk and make a mayonnaise by adding the olive oil a little at a time, whisking constantly.
2. As the sauce thickens, add a little lemon juice, then oil, then juice, etc., until completely incorporated into the sauce. Once all the oil has been added, add the Tabasco and correct the seasoning.

Here is a recipe very typically prepared in the South of France. It was first served in our restaurant as a special request, and, to this day, customers who love it call in and order it in advance.

CHIFFONNADE DE SCAROLE

This is leaf of escarole served with a traditional French vinaigrette.

FILLET DE BOEUF À LA FICELLE
ENTOURÉ DE SES LEGUMES—SAUCE BÉARNAISE

2 pounds tenderloin of beef,
   trimmed of fat and tied
   up with twine
6 teaspoons coarse salt
1 green cabbage
4 carrots
4 leeks

4 turnips
1 large onion
   Bouquet garni
   (thyme and parsley)
2 cloves garlic
   BÉARNAISE SAUCE
   (see index)

1. Lay the tenderloin of beef in a deep dish 2 hours prior to the cooking and sprinkle 2 teaspoons coarse salt all over the meat. Let the meat stand in the refrigerator.
2. Cut the cabbage in quarters and remove the hard core. Wash, trim, and peel the carrots, leeks, turnips, and onion. Set aside.
3. Half fill a deep stock pan with water. Add 4 teaspoons of coarse salt and put on medium heat. Add the bouquet garni, the onion, and the garlic cloves. Let it boil for 30 minutes.
4. Add all the vegetables, let the boiling start again, but then lower the heat and simmer for 20 minutes.
5. Add the tenderloin after bringing liquid to a boil again, count 11 minutes, and remove from heat.
6. To serve, untie the beef and slice. On each dinner plate, attractively arrange 2 slices of tenderloin, 1 carrot, 1 leek, 1 turnip, and 1 quarter of cabbage. Serve with Béarnaise Sauce.

BRIE DE MEAUX ET VIEUX CHAUMES

These fine cheeses may be found in a gourmet cheese shop. Arrange attractively on a serving platter.

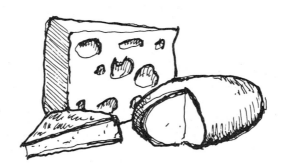

MARQUISE AU CHOCOLAT DU YA CA

*12 ounces European
bittersweet chocolate
6 ounces butter*

*5 eggs
3 ounces sugar
CRÊME ANGLAISE*

1. In a *bain marie,* melt the bittersweet chocolate with the butter until very smooth. Set aside.
2. Separate the yolks from the whites. Whisk the yolks with sugar until foamy white.
3. Whisk the whites of egg until stiff.
4. While the chocolate mixture is still luke warm, mix it with the yolks. Then, with a wooden spoon, delicately blend in the egg whites.
5. Butter a mold. Pour the preparation into the mold and put it in a freezer for a minimum of 5 hours. Take out of the freezer 1 hour prior to serving.
6. Serve it sliced on a plate covered with Crême Anglaise.

   *I have given the measurements in weight because it is more precise that way, and this recipe **must** be precise.*

LE YA CA

CRÊME ANGLAISE

2 cups milk	6 egg yolks
1½ teaspoons vanilla extract	6 tablespoons sugar

1. Scald the milk with the vanilla in a heavy medium-size saucepan.
2. Beat the egg yolks and sugar together in a mixing bowl until pale in color and the mixture forms a ribbon when the whisk is lifted.
3. In a second, heavy enameled saucepan, heat the egg mixture over low heat stirring constantly with a wooden spoon. Gradually add the hot milk, continuing to stir. Continue to cook over low heat, stirring until the mixture thickens and will coat a metal spoon (about 165° on a candy thermometer). The mixture must not be allowed to boil. Immediately remove from the heat and pour into a cold container.
4. When thoroughly cool, cover the container and refrigerate until serving time.

*This is **the** dessert that made our restaurant famous in France. We have served it for 21 years.*

The Lighthouse
Oceanfront

Dinner for Four

Steamed Clams and Crabmeat Cocktail

Crab Cakes

Steamed Shrimp

Stuffed Flounder

Scallops

Rum Cake with Sauce

German Chocolate Pie

Beverages:

With Appetizers—Bloody Mary

With Main Courses—Pouilly Fuisse

Robert Herman, Proprietor

Clint Stephenson, Chef

THE LIGHTHOUSE

In 1963 The Lighthouse was taken over by the present owner, Robert Herman. The menu at that time included mainly hot dogs, hamburgers, steamed/fried shrimp, hard shell crabs, and frosted mugs of beer. The restaurant could seat 26 people. With the development of the south end of Virginia Beach, especially Rudee Inlet, The Lighthouse was forced to expand. With long lines forming, the ownership began in the 1970's to add a room each year. Now in the 1980's, approximately 550 people can be accommodated.

All of the seafood is delivered fresh daily, inventoried, and ordered each evening after the dinner hour. The kitchen orders for only one day at a time. Breads and desserts are baked on the premises. Anniversary, birthday, and special occasion baked goods are a specialty.

The Lighthouse is open year round, catering to local customers during the off-season and to tourists in the summer. Most of the key employees have been with the organization for many years. "The secret to our success," says Robert Herman, "is preparing the freshest, finest local seafood with classic recipes that enhance the flavor of the seafood." The phenomenal growth over the past 20 years is testimony to the extraordinary quality of this special restaurant.

First and Atlantic Avenue   428-9851
Virginia Beach

STEAMED CLAMS

4 dozen nick clams
½ cup butter

White pepper
2 lemons, juiced

1. Wash the clams well and place in a covered pan of boiling water. As soon as the clams open, approximately 10 minutes, remove from the water and take out of the shells.
2. Melt the butter, sprinkle with white pepper, and squeeze the lemon juice into the hot butter.
3. Dip the clams in the butter for a delicious appetizer.

Nick clams are a size smaller than Cherrystones and much more tender.

CRABMEAT COCKTAIL

1 pound Backfin crabmeat
Lettuce

Lemon wedges
Cocktail sauce

1. Remove the lumps from the crabmeat but don't break up. Look for tiny shells to remove.
2. Decoratively place the crabmeat on a bed of lettuce with plenty of lemon and cocktail sauce.

Deluxe Backfin crabmeat is the finest available.

CRAB CAKES

1 teaspoon mustard	1 teaspoon Worcestershire sauce
1 teaspoon mayonnaise	
¼ teaspoon baking powder	1½ pounds Backfin crabmeat
2 eggs, beaten	White pepper
3 teaspoons chopped parsley	1 tablespoon lemon juice
¼ teaspoon seafood seasoning	Salt, to taste
1 teaspoon chopped pimentos	1 cup bread crumbs

1. Combine all ingredients, adding bread crumbs last.
2. Form into 8 large cakes and bake at 350° for 15 minutes.

Crabcakes make a wonderful snack or can be served for a special luncheon treat.

STEAMED SHRIMP

2 cans beer	Seafood seasoning
1½ cups vinegar	Juice of 2 lemons
Bay leaves	24 (12/15 count) shrimp

1. Bring the beer, vinegar, bay leaves, a sprinkle of seasoning, and the lemon juice to a boil.
2. Add the shrimp and cook for approximately 4 minutes.
3. Remove and sprinkle seafood seasoning on top.

It is possible that we sell more shrimp than anyone in the state. For 21 years our Steamed Shrimp has been one of our most popular menu items.

THE LIGHTHOUSE

STUFFED FLOUNDER

4 whole Fluke flounder	Juice of 1 lemon
1 pound Backfin crabmeat	Seafood seasoning
½ teaspoon white pepper	¼ cup butter, melted

1. Fillet the flounder, using both sides.
2. Mix the crabmeat with the white pepper, juice of ½ lemon, and just a sprinkling of seafood seasoning.
3. Mound the stuffing between the two fillets of each fish, like a sandwich, and baste with a mixture of butter and remaining lemon juice.
4. Bake at 350° for approximately 18 minutes.

Fluke flounder is the best quality flounder available, and we are very fortunate that it is native to the waters of the Chesapeake.

SCALLOPS

24 large ocean scallops	Juice of 2 lemons
¼ cup dry white wine	¼ cup melted butter
¼ teaspoon white pepper	Paprika

1. Wash all grit from the scallops. Place in a baking dish and cover with the white wine, pepper, and lemon juice.
2. Bake for approximately 15 minutes at 350°, basting several times with melted butter.
3. Sprinkle very lightly with paprika at the end of cooking and serve.

We insist on the freshest possible seafood. We buy our scallops right off the boats.

RUM CAKE

½ cup chopped pecans
1 package yellow cake mix
   (Duncan Hines)
1 (3-ounce) package vanilla
   instant pudding mix
½ cup vegetable oil

½ cup rum
½ cup water
4 eggs
  Vanilla ice cream
  RUM SAUCE
  Whipped cream
  Maraschino cherries

1. Grease and flour a bundt pan.
2. Sprinkle pecans in the bottom of the pan.
3. Combine the cake mix, pudding mix, oil, rum, water, and eggs. Pour the batter over the pecans in the pan.
4. Bake at 325° for 45-55 minutes.
5. Remove the cake from the pan and place it on a plate to cool.
6. To serve, place 2 slices of cake on a serving dish, top with a scoop of vanilla ice cream, Rum Sauce, and garnish with whipped cream and a maraschino cherry.

RUM SAUCE

½ cup butter
1 cup sugar

¼ cup rum
¼ cup water

Melt the butter in a saucepan and add the sugar, stirring until dissolved. Add the rum and water, stirring until well blended.

This is probably our most popular dessert. It is our House Specialty.

GERMAN CHOCOLATE PIE

3 eggs
1 cup sugar
3 tablespoons flour
½ cup margarine

¾ bar of German Chocolate
1 teaspoon vanilla
1 cup chopped pecans
Coconut

1. Beat the eggs well, then add the sugar. Mix in the flour and beat well again.
2. Meanwhile, melt the margarine and chocolate together. Add the vanilla and cool.
3. Pour the chocolate mixture into the egg mixture and beat well. Add the pecans and pour into a greased 9-inch pie plate. Sprinkle with coconut.
4. Bake at 350° for 30-40 minutes. Cool thoroughly before serving.

This dessert freezes very well.

Lockhart's
of Norfolk

Dinner for Four

Classic Milk Oyster Stew

Hot Spiced Shrimp

Summer Salad

Flounder Mediterranean

Scottish Boiled Potatoes and Special Stewed Tomatoes

Brandied Peaches

Beverages:

Apertif—Harvey's Medium Dry Amontillodo Sherry

Pinkus Weizen Beer

Samuel Smith's Old Brewery Pale Ale

Johnny Lockhart, Proprietor and Chef

LOCKHART'S OF NORFOLK

Lockhart's of Norfolk, gourmet seafood restaurant, is celebrating 25 years of service to the Tidewater area. From its origin in 1959 as a neighborhood tavern to its present day modern kitchen and gourmet preparations, the freshest local seafood obtainable has always been served. For the real beginning of the Lockhart food serving tradition, one must reach back into the 1930's, a time when Norfolk supported the colorful City Market. Grandma Lockhart operated the Brewer Street Café amidst all the noisy activities, attracting people to her country home cooking and lively manners. Her day commenced early, searching every stall in the City Market. The seafood, beef, poultry, and vegetables brought in fresh each morning would soon be carried to her café and prepared into fabulous hot meals.

Johnny Lockhart, imaginative chef of Lockhart's, grew up with this background of serving people fresh seafood and vegetables, so it was natural for him to launch a native restaurant. It began as the Neighborhood Inn, a local tavern serving sandwiches, crab cakes on crackers, and spicy deviled crabs. This expanded in the mid-1960's to the Crab House, centered around steamed crabs cooked in huge boiling pots and served with pitchers of draught beer and summer salads. Johnny added two or three new dishes every year to his growing menu, holding steadfast to a method of using seafood freshly caught in local waters. Oysters Ghent, Hot Pots, Flounder Mediterranean, Oysters '76, Poach Broiling, Cloud Light Frying, and Super Sauton Picasso—a colorful blend of seafood and herbs—were all successful and are a part of the menu today. One hundred selections of world beers and an extensive wine list organized by J. T. Lockhart, resident wine sommelier, have been added to the bill of fare. "We have found that each beer and wine has a unique flavor all its own and is perfectly compatible with whatever seafood you have selected," says J. T. Lockhart.

With springtime comes gardening season, and, as his grandmother did, Johnny begins his restaurant garden every year. The entire family tends a large tree-shaded plot beside the restaurant. The summer salads are home grown, and the new herb boxes provide fresh aromatic herbs to heighten the flavor of seafood. The entire Lockhart family works together, just as in the old days of the Brewer Street Café, sharing with everyone fresh local seafood, herbs, and vegetables that make life so much more enjoyable.

8440 Tidewater Drive   588-0405
Norfolk

CLASSIC MILK OYSTER STEW

16 oysters with juice
4 tablespoons butter

2 cups half & half
Paprika

1. Cook the oysters and juice with butter in a saucepan until boiling, then decrease heat to a simmer.
2. Stir in the cream slowly until steaming hot, being careful not to boil.
3. Garnish with paprika.

For twenty-five years this stew has been a favorite of our customers. The secret of this recipe is to serve it immediately after it is prepared. It should not be made in advance.

HOT SPICED SHRIMP

16 shrimp, peeled and
    deveined
16 ounces Pinkus Weizen Beer
2 cups water
    Juice of 2 whole lemons
4 teaspoons Old Bay
    Seasoning

1 teaspoon salt
1 teaspoon pepper
    Dash of Tabasco
    Lemon wedges, for garnish
    Parsley, for garnish

1. Combine the shrimp with all the remaining ingredients except the garnishes and cook until done.
2. Serve the hot liquid in bowls. Garnish with lemon wedges and sprigs of parsley.

The beer in this recipe makes it very unusual. Prepare this appetizer just before serving.

SUMMER SALAD

2 tomatoes, cut in wedges
2 cucumbers, sliced in strips
2 green peppers, chopped
8 spring onions

Various fresh herbs
Freshly picked vegetables
WINE AND VINEGAR
DRESSING

Wash and prepare the garden vegetables and serve with Wine and Vinegar Dressing.

WINE AND VINEGAR DRESSING

10 ounces wine vinegar
10 ounces Chablis wine
¼ teaspoon celery salt

¼ teaspoon crushed pepper
½ teaspoon Salad Supreme
Spices

Combine all ingredients.

All of the herbs and salad ingredients used in the recipes at Lockhart's are grown in our own garden.

FLOUNDER MEDITERRANEAN

4 (10-ounce) flounder fillets
½ cup olive oil
½ cup white wine
½ cup butter

½ cup chopped parsley
4 teaspoons oregano
1 cup chopped onion
8 garlic cloves, chopped

1. Place the flounder in a shallow baking dish which has been sprayed with a non-stick vegetable oil. Top with all the ingredients.
2. Poach on a flame until half done, then poach under the broiler until brown on top and soft inside. Pour off any excess liquid before serving.
3. Serve with Scottish Boiled Potatoes and Special Stewed Tomatoes.

I recieved this recipe from a Mediterranean friend over twenty years ago. Flounder Mediterranean *has been served in our restaurant since that time, and we have never found a person who doesn't like it.*

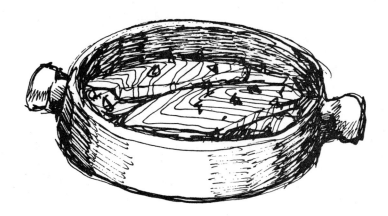

SCOTTISH BOILED POTATOES

4 *potatoes*   *Celery salt*
1½ *cubes butter*

Boil one potato per person, whole, in water, adding ¼ stick butter per potato. When done, quarter the potato lengthwise, top with more butter, and add a dash of celery salt.

SPECIAL STEWED TOMATOES

8 *whole tomatoes*   1 *teaspoon basil*
1 *teaspoon sugar*   4 *teaspoons butter*
½ *teaspoon tarragon*

Scald the tomatoes, peel, and place in a saucepan and crush. Cook on medium heat until soft. Mix in remaining ingredients. Stew until done.

BRANDIED PEACHES

8 large, fancy peach halves
1⅓ ounces peach brandy
1 ounce brandy
   Dash of ginger
   Dash of cinnamon

1 tablespoon simple syrup
   (mix 1 tablespoon sugar
   and 1 tablespoon water)
4 whole, stemmed
   maraschino cherries
   Whipped cream

1. Put the peach halves in a container; add the peach brandy, brandy, ginger, cinnamon, and simple syrup. Cover and let marinate for at least 24 hours.
2. Remove the peaches from the marinade and place a half in each serving dish. Spoon over some of the syrup. Top with a cherry and whipped cream.

Dinner for Four

Clam Chowder

Mediterranean Salad
with Feta Cheese Dressing

Shrimp à la Greque
with Black Beans and Rice

Belgium Whiskey Pudding

Wine:

Domestica, Greece
(Crisp, dry unique character)

Thomas and Christopher Kyrus, Proprietors

Samih Husein, Chef

LYNNHAVEN FISH HOUSE

Virginia Beach, one of Tidewater's newest, largest, and fastest growing cities, is the home of the young, but ever-popular, Lynnhaven Fish House Restaurant. This haven for lovers of seafood is the on-going challenge of owners Thomas C. Kyrus, and his son Christopher. Nestled on the shore of the alluring Chesapeake Bay, the view from the dining area offers the romance of a beachfront dining experience touched by the silhouette of the adjoining Lynnhaven Fishing Pier and the graceful lines of the famous Chesapeake Bay Bridge-Tunnel in the not-too-distant background. Drawing upon his years of experience in operating his own real estate business, a people-oriented profession, Mr. Kyrus has skillfully considered and met the needs of this area by providing one of the finest seafood restaurants on the East Coast. Whether dining while on business or for pleasure, the relaxed and quiet atmosphere and remarkable menu, entwined with service reminiscent of Southern hospitality, creates within the customer the feeling that he or she has found a special place, indeed.

The menu features vast offerings ranging from succulent shellfish appetizers and unusual salads and soups to gourmet seafood entrées and basic "old favorites," with a modest selection of the finest beef. The dessert menu features, among other offerings, a Belgium Whiskey Pudding that is irresistible. Each item is skillfully and distinctively prepared by Chef Samih Husein, who has a flair for creating sauces to delight the most ardent gourmet. "Chef Samih," as he is known to all who have sampled his culinary seafood triumphs, is able to bring forth an artful presentation that is unsurpassed. With a potpourri culinary background, he has a wealth of experience and skill to draw upon to please the most discerning diner. Chef Samih was one of the twelve chefs selected statewide to represent the Lynnhaven Fish House Restaurant as a sampling of this city's finer seafood restaurants at a seafood presentation, entitled "The Great Taste of Virginia Seafood," in September 1983.

A spirit of teamwork exists within the framework of Lynnhaven Fish House Restaurant's operation. All work together toward a common goal—providing customers with a comfortable, totally satisfying, and pleasurable dining experience. The entire staff works diligently toward keeping the fine reputation the Lynnhaven Fish House Restaurant has earned.

2350 Starfish Road   481-0003
Virginia Beach

LYNNHAVEN FISH HOUSE

CLAM CHOWDER

½ pound bacon
1 clove garlic, minced
2 tablespoons olive oil
1 medium onion, diced
4 stalks celery, diced
2 medium potatoes, diced
1 medium carrot, diced
2 medium tomatoes, diced
½ pound fresh clams, chopped (reserve juice)

4 cups clam juice or chicken stock
½ teaspoon oregano
½ teaspoon thyme
½ teaspoon sweet basil
1 bay leaf
Salt and pepper, to taste
2 tablespoons flour or 2 teaspoons cornstarch

1. Fry the bacon until crisp; reserve the drippings. Drain the bacon, dice, and set aside.
2. In a heavy saucepan, over medium heat, brown the minced garlic in the olive oil and reserved bacon drippings.
3. Add the vegetables and sauté lightly.
4. Add the fresh, chopped clams, stock or clam juice, bacon and all remaining ingredients except the flour or cornstarch. Cook over medium heat until the clams are tender.
5. Thicken the stock with flour or cornstarch and serve piping hot.

MEDITERRANEAN SALAD

An abundance of fresh greens in addition to shrimp, artichokes mushrooms, Feta cheese, sardines, anchovies, black olives, hearts of palm, beets, tomatoes, and chick peas give this salad its Mediterranean character. Play with it—perhaps you like more sardines than I—make it a creation of your imagination and desires.

FETA CHEESE DRESSING

8 ounces Feta cheese
4 ounces sour cream
¼ cup mayonnaise
1 tablespoon olive oil

1 teaspoon vinegar
1 teaspoon Worcestershire
   sauce
Salt and pepper, to taste

In a large bowl, combine all ingredients and mix well. Let stand for 2 hours in the refrigerator before serving over the salad.

This dressing provides the perfect final taste for your salad creation.

SHRIMP Á LA GREQUE

2 tablespoons butter
2 tablespoons olive oil
1 clove garlic, minced
1 medium onion, chopped
2 whole pepperoncini, minced
4 whole green olives, chopped
2 whole black, Greek olives, chopped
1 medium tomato, sliced

½ cup crushed tomato
4 ounces Feta cheese, crumbled
Pinch of fresh parsley
Pinch of oregano
Salt and pepper, to taste
24 medium shrimp, peeled and deveined
4 tablespoons Greek white wine
Rice Pilaf

1. Melt the butter and add the olive oil.
2. Add all the other ingredients except the shrimp and wine to the butter and olive oil and sauté.
3. After the mixture is sautéed, add the shrimp. Cook over medium heat for approximately 5 minutes.
4. Add the wine and continue heating for an additional 2 or 3 minutes.
5. Serve over Rice Pilaf, or any rice variation, as desired.

I love adding Mediterranean flavors to the seafoods of this area to make totally new recipes. This one is a customer favorite.

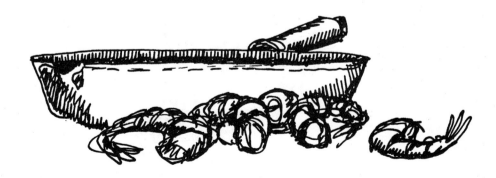

LYNNHAVEN FISH HOUSE

BLACK BEANS

2 cups black beans
½ cup minced onion
½ cup minced green pepper
½ cup red wine vinegar
1 pound smoked ham bone
   or smoked ham

2 tablespoons butter
3 tablespoons olive oil
1 clove fresh minced garlic
1 bay leaf
1 teaspoon thyme leaves
   Salt and pepper, to taste

1. Rinse and clean the beans and soak in plain water (or beef, chicken, or ham stock) overnight.
2. Cook the beans for 1 hour until soft.
3. Add all the other ingredients and cook further (over medium heat) until the beans become very soft, taking care not to mash.
4. To thicken, mix 2 tablespoons all-purpose flour in water and add to the beans (mixing through gently) just before serving hot.
5. Serve over cooked white rice, if desired.

This recipe serves six to eight people.

Although typically Southern, this dish has a touch of Mediterranean and combines surprisingly well as a side dish with other recipes.

BELGIUM WHISKEY PUDDING

2½ cups all-purpose flour
    or 3 cups cake flour
3½ teaspoons baking powder
2 cups sugar
1 teaspoon salt
1 teaspoon cinnamon
¼ cup shortening

½ cup milk
1 teaspoon vanilla
3 tablespoons whiskey
1 tablespoon rum
3 whole eggs
2 egg yolks
Whipped cream
Nuts, for garnish

1. Heat oven to 350°, grease and flour baking pans (round 8"-9" pans preferred, but any shape may be used if it has comparable dimensions).
2. In a large mixing bowl, combine the flour, baking powder, sugar, salt, cinnamon, shortening, milk, vanilla, whiskey, and rum.
3. Blend 1 minute on low speed, scraping the bowl constantly.
4. In a separate bowl, beat the whole eggs and the two additional egg yolks together.
5. Add the beaten eggs to the flour mixture and beat 2 additional minutes on high speed, remembering to again scrape the bowl.
6. Pour into pans. Bake round layers for 30-35 minutes, oblong 35-40 minutes—or until a wooden pick inserted in the center comes out clean.
7. Scoop into serving cups or tall, tapered glasses.
8. Top with whipped cream and your favorite nuts.

The flavor of this irresistible pudding tops off the meal. It is a finale to relax with.

MASTER'S

Dinner for Four

Turtle Soup

Crab Byron

Veal Madeira

Raspberry Sorbet

Chapon Salad

Strawberries Master's

Beverages:
Aperitif—Kir Royale
With Turtle Soup and Crab Bryon—Sonoma Vineyards Chardonnay
With Veal Madeira—Chateau Larose Trintaudon
With Strawberries Master's—Codorniu Blanc de Blanc

Linda T. Chappell, Proprietor
Chip Fraser and Pamela Fuller, General Managers
Jay Blair, Chef
Victor Janciukas, Maitre 'd

From 1934 to 1974, Master's Drug Store stood on the corner of West Princess Anne Road. It was a popular meeting spot, and many a soda was sipped at the fountain. After Master's Drug store closed, several restaurants occupied the space until, finally, on Febuary 19, 1984, Master's restaurant found a home there and opened to rave reviews. Justly famed for the authenicity of its classic cuisine and the originality of its menu, Master's has become synonymous with extraordinary food and unique presentation, set in a classic yet warm atmosphere, in the Ghent section of Norfolk.

Chef Jay Blair, known for his remarkable culinary talents, has brought to Tidewater a touch of New Orleans. His ability to combine the French aesthetic with a distinctive American flavor has created a repertoire of incomparable dishes. Serving the discerning palate, Master's is mindful of the freshness and seasonal availability of ingredients. Its inventive menu accentuates sauces and additionally offers a *prix-fixe* dinner for the guests who look forward to a culinary adventure. Complimenting the cuisine, Master's offers a wine list of exceptional value and vintage.

Chip Fraser sums up the goals of Master's owner and staff: "We want people to walk out and remember the meal they have had so they will want to come back again and again. We strive to serve excellent and creative food, properly presented in an unsurpassed atmosphere."

749 West Princess Anne Road   627-4293
Norfolk

MASTER'S

TURTLE SOUP

½ medium onion,
 finely chopped
2 stalks celery,
 finely chopped
1 tablespoon whole thyme
1 oregano
3 bay leaves
½ pound fillet of turtle meat,
 coarsely ground

2 quarts beef and lobster
 stock, combined
3 tablespoons flour
½ cup water
½ cup chopped spinach
2 hard-cooked eggs,
 finely chopped
2 lemons, rind grated and
 juice reserved
¼ cup dry sherry

1. In a saucepan sauté the chopped onions, celery, thyme, oregano, and bay leaves with the turtle meat, cooking slowly over medium heat for 45 minutes to an hour, stirring frequently. Add the stock and bring to a boil.
2. Make a *white wash* by combining the flour and the water, stirring constantly for a smooth consistency. Strain slowly into the pan, again stirring constantly. Cook for 15 minutes.
3. Add the chopped spinach, eggs, lemon rind, lemon juice, and sherry. Serve immediately.

Turtle meat is available on the East Coast, specifically in Maryland and in the Florida Keys.

This is a rich soup with a Cajun twang. It is a real touch of New Orleans.

CRAB BYRON

1 cup Chablis wine
1 tablespoon whole thyme
2 bay leaves
2 tablespoons butter
3 tablespoons chopped onion

3 tablespoons chopped celery
1 pound lump crabmeat
2 tablespoons seafood
  velouté
¾ cup bread crumbs

1. In a small saucepan, combine the wine, thyme, and bay leaves and reduce over high heat to ½ cup. Set aside.
2. In a sauté pan, melt the butter and sauté the onion and celery until tender. Add the crabmeat (being careful not to break it up).
3. Strain the reduction into the crabmeat, adding the velouté, saving ¼ cup for the top.
4. Place the mixture in four 3¾-ounce soufflé cups, top with bread crumbs, and bake at 350° for 10 minutes. Serve.

This crab appetizer is hot and spicy and a wonderful preface to a meal.

VEAL MADEIRA

¼ cup glacé de veau
¾ pound butter
2 lemons
8 (3-ounce) veal loin
   medallions
  Flour
2 tablespoons cottonseed oil

¼ cup Madeira wine
¾ cup sliced fresh mushrooms
¼ cup capers
¾ cup artichoke hearts
   (remove chokes)
16 steamed snow peas,
  for garnish

1. To make the lemon butter, put the *glacé de veau* in a sauté pan over low heat. Whisk in the butter, whisking constantly to avoid clarification of the butter. Remove from the heat, then add the juice from the lemons and set aside.

2. Lightly dust the veal with flour. Sauté the veal in cottonseed oil. Cook to desired doneness and remove from the pan. Deglaze the pan with the Madeira wine. Add the sliced mushrooms, capers, and artichoke hearts. Cook over high heat for 30 seconds and remove from the heat.

3. Add the lemon butter mixture and spoon over the medallions of veal. Garnish with steamed snow peas and serve.

At Master's, the entrée which the waiter brings to the diner is actually a plate painting. Each meal is an artistic presentation of sauces arranged on the plate to create an appealing and attractive visual impression.

RASPBERRY SORBET

⅔ cup sugar
3 cups water
1 pint raspberries

2 tablespoons fresh lemon juice
4 tablespoons sweet vermouth
4 tablespoons Chambord

1. Dissolve the sugar in the water over heat and set aside.
2. Purée and strain the raspberries.
3. Combine the raspberries, lemon juice, vermoth, and Chambord and freeze until crystalized.
4. Stir the mixture 2 times at ½ hour intervals, re-freezing each time. Serve in small, stemmed glasses, frosting the rims with sugar.

This sorbet cleanses the palate. It should be served after the entrée and before the salad.

CHAPON SALAD

½ head Boston lettuce
½ head romaine
⅓ bunch endive
1 bunch watercress
½ bunch spinach

OIL AND VINEGAR DRESSING
½ cup cooked bacon, crumbled
4 large mushrooms, sliced
Croutons

1. Wash, dry, and prepare the salad greens.
2. Place the greens in a large salad bowl and toss with the Oil and Vinegar Dressing.
3. Place the tossed greens on four chilled salad plates, and sprinkle 2 tablespoons of bacon, 1 sliced mushroom, and croutons over the top of each salad.

OIL AND VINEGAR DRESSING

¼ cup vinegar
¾ cup oil

1 small clove garlic, mashed
¼ teaspoon dry mustard
Salt and pepper, to taste

Combine all ingredients and mix thoroughly.

STRAWBERRIES MASTER'S

1 pound cream cheese
¼ cup sour cream
1 tablespoon granulated
   sugar
¼ cup heavy whipping cream

½ teaspoon vanilla
1 tablespoon Crème
   de Noyaux
1 quart fresh strawberries,
   cleaned and stemmed
Fresh mint, for garnish

1. Combine the cream cheese, sour cream, sugar, cream, vanilla, and Crème de Noyaux to make a sauce.
2. Place the strawberries in four champagne glasses and pour the sauce over the top. Garnish with sprigs of mint.

The combination of the strawberries with this sauce is heavenly. It is a fine way to end the evening.

Milton Warren's

Ice House Restaurant
...of Virginia Beach

Dinner for Eight

Oyster and Spinach Bisque

*Garden Green Salad with Sliced Peeled Tomatoes
with Ice House Dressing*

*Roast Rack of Spring Lamb
with Mint Jelly and Chutney*

Rice with an Eastern Flare

Fresh Green Beans

Hot Popovers

*Milton Warren's Ice House Restaurant
Cheesecake*

Wine:

Kenwood Zinfandel, Sonoma Valley

Milton Warren and Sally Warren, Proprietors

Tom Harp, Food Service Manager and Chef

MILTON WARREN'S ICE HOUSE

Milton Warren's Ice House is warm now. An actual converted ice house, the atmosphere is inviting and reminiscent of a country inn.

Built at the turn of the century, this sturdy brick building served as Virginia Beach's first and, for many years, only ice house. Originally aiding the local fishing industry, it was expanded to supply cottages and hotels as the resort area grew. After succumbing to the advance of the electric refrigerator, the Ice House closed its doors to be reborn, on May 13, 1976, as Milton Warren's Ice House Restaurant.

Today it is run by Milton Warren, his daughter Sally Warren, along with Tom Harp, the food service manager and chef. The menu has varied little over the years. Fresh local seafood, fresh vegetables from the farm, and popovers have become trademarks. The reviews have been outstanding. Milton Warren takes a personal interest in each guest and continues to live up to the fine reputation his restaurant enjoys.

604 Norfolk Avenue   422-2323
Virginia Beach

OYSTER AND SPINACH BISQUE

1 (10-ounce) package frozen, chopped spinach
½ pound butter
1 cup chopped onion
2-3 cloves garlic, chopped
1 pint standard oysters

1 tablespoon chicken base
½ cup flour
1 quart half & half
Salt, to taste
White pepper, to taste
Cooking sherry, to taste

1. Cook the spinach and drain. Place it in a food processor and chop. (Do not purée.)
2. In a large saucepan, melt half of the butter. Sauté the onion and garlic, add the oysters, cooking slightly or until the edges of the oysters curl. Remove from the heat, put into the food processor, and chop. (Do not purée.)
3. In the same saucepan, melt the remaining butter and chicken base, add flour slowly, and, stirring constantly, add the half & half slowly. Stirring constantly to prevent lumping, cook until smooth. Add the chopped spinach and continue stirring. Add the oysters, salt, pepper, and sherry, continuing to stir until all ingredients are blended. Remove from heat; cool.
4. Refrigerate for at least 4 hours before serving. For best results, refrigerate overnight. Reheat only the amount to be used.

To enhance the flavor of our Oyster and Spinach Bisque, add a small amount of cream sherry just before serving.

GARDEN GREEN SALAD with SLICED PEELED TOMATOES with ICE HOUSE DRESSING

1 *head romaine*	1 *head Boston lettuce*
1 *head leaf lettuce*	4 *firm, ripe tomatoes*

1. Separate and clean the lettuce, then place in cool water for 1 hour. Drain and place in the refrigerator.
2. Place the tomatoes in a collander and immerse in boiling water for 10 seconds, then immerse in ice water and let cool, and then refrigerate.
3. Tear the lettuce, do not cut, and mix all three together. Place on individual plates.
4. Slip the tomato skins off and slice. Place on top of the lettuce.

ICE HOUSE SALAD DRESSING

1 small onion,
    cut into eighths
½ teaspoon salt
½ teaspoon pepper
1 tablespoon lemon juice
1 tablespoon soy sauce
1 tablespoon Worcestershire
    sauce
3-4 drops Tabasco (optional)

1 large egg
1½ quarts (approximately)
    peanut oil
1 cup parsley (fresh or dry),
    finely chopped
1 (16-ounce) carton
    sour cream
2 cups buttermilk

1. Place all the ingredients except for the peanut oil, parsley, sour cream, and buttermilk in a food processor and chop until smooth, turning the processor on and off.
2. With the processor running, add the peanut oil very, very slowly in a small stream, until the dressing is the consistency of mayonnaise.
3. Place the parsley, sour cream, and buttermilk in the large bowl of an electric mixer. Slowly add the processed ingredients until well blended.
4. For best results, refrigerate the dressing for at least 1 day before using.

This amount of dressing will serve more than eight people; however, it is delicious, it keeps well in the refrigerator, and you will be very happy to have it on hand.

ROAST RACK OF SPRING LAMB

4 *racks of lamb*
   Butter, melted
   Salt and pepper
   Basil, thyme, and
      rosemary

Fresh garlic slices
Mint jelly
Chutney

1. Have the butcher cut the chime bone out of the rack of lamb and cut 2 inches off of the ribs to even it up.
2. Peel off all the fat. Trim tendons and trim between the ribs. All fat should be removed.
3. Place the racks in a roasting pan. Baste each rack with melted butter, then salt and pepper. Season with basil, thyme, rosemary, and fresh garlic slices on each rack.
4. Roast for 10 minutes at 350°. Remove from the oven and let rest for 5 minutes. Return to the oven for 2 minutes, remove, and slice between the ribs.
5. Serve 4 ribs per person with mint jelly and chutney.

As an added touch when serving lamb, place paper frills on each rib before serving.

RICE WITH AN EASTERN FLARE

Rice, uncooked
Butter
1 tablespoon chicken base
2 cups chopped onions
2 cups chopped celery

2 cups chopped green peppers
2 tablespoons soy sauce
Salt and pepper
Pimentos
Sliced toasted almonds

1. Cook the rice according to package directions for 4-6 servings. Add to the water 1 tablespoon of butter and the chicken base.
2. Sauté the onions, celery, and green peppers in butter and soy sauce. Add salt and pepper to taste.
3. Mix the cooked rice and vegetables in a baking dish. Garnish with sliced pimentos and almonds. Cover and place in warm oven (300°).

GREEN BEANS

4 cups water	Salt and pepper, to taste
4 tablespoons butter	3 pounds green beans

1. Boil the water seasoned with the butter and salt and pepper to taste.
2. Wash and snap off the ends of the green beans. Place in a collander and immerse in boiling water. Let cook approximately 15 minutes or until desired tenderness is reached.

HOT POPOVERS

8 eggs	1 teaspoon salt
1 quart milk	3 cups flour, sifted
4 teaspoons butter, melted	Peanut oil

1. All ingredients should be at room temperature.
2. Mix the eggs, milk, butter, and salt until smooth. Add the sifted flour and mix only enough to make smooth.
3. Grease muffin pan with peanut oil: no more than ⅓ teaspoon per cup. Heat in the oven. Fill each cup of hot muffin pan with batter until ⅔ full.
4. Bake at 450° for 30 minutes. Reduce heat to 350° and bake an additional 15 minutes without opening the oven. If not completely brown, cook a little longer.

MILTON WARREN'S ICE HOUSE RESTAURANT
CHEESECAKE

CRUST:
- 1 (14-ounce) package vanilla wafers
- 4 teaspoons sugar
- 4 teaspoons butter
- 1 teaspoon vanilla

FILLING:
- 3 (8-ounce) packages cream cheese
- 2 cups sugar
- 5 eggs
- 2 teaspoons vanilla

TOPPING:
- 1 pint sour cream
- ½ cup sugar
- 2 teaspoons vanilla

1. CRUST: Mix all the Crust ingredients in a blender, then press evenly into a 9-inch springform pan, bottom and sides.
2. FILLING: Mix all the Filling ingredients in a blender until smooth. Pour into the crust and bake for 1½ hours at 325°. Cool slightly.
3. TOPPING: Mix all the Topping ingredients in a blender until smooth. Spread on the cooled filling and bake for another 15 minutes. Cool, then place in the refrigerator for 24 hours before serving.

Phillips

Dinner for Four

Clams Casino

Onion Soup Gratinée

Garden Salad

Scallops Florentine

Key Lime Pie

Phillips Waterside Coffee

Wine:

Mouton Cadet Blanc

*Brice, Shirley, Steve, Olivia,
and Jeff Phillips, Proprietors*

Eugene Preston, Chef

Buzz Joseph, General Manager

When Shirley and Brice Phillips came to Ocean City, Maryland, with their two young sons in 1957, Ocean City was a small resort town opening its season on Memorial Day and shutting its doors for the winter on Labor Day. The small shack they purchased for a carry-out shop "up the beach" at 20th Street was to serve a dual purpose. First, it was an ideal outlet to sell crabs and crabmeat which were in surplus supply from the family's seafood packing plant on Hooper's Island in Chesapeake Bay. Secondly, the young couple imagined leisurely days spent on the beach with their sons, Steve and Jeffrey. The first season put those dreams to rest as business expanded rapidly and long hours were required to lay the foundation for Phillips as it is today.

By 1967, Phillips Crab House had expanded to four kitchens and nine dining rooms. Today, Phillips Crab House boasts a seating capacity of 1400 and a staff of more than 400 employees. In 1973, the introduction of a second location in Ocean City added a new dimension to dining with Phillips. Phillips by the Sea is located in the Phillips Beach Plaza Hotel and serves traditional favorites in an elegant and relaxed dining room overlooking the ocean. Two more Maryland locations followed, Phillips Seafood House and Phillips Harborplace, before Phillips Waterside opened on June 1, 1983, in Norfolk, Virginia, to serve the people of the Tidewater area.

Twenty-seven years have now passed since the Shirley and Brice began "up the beach." "We predict continued growth under the direction of Steve, Olivia, and Jeff Phillips and our devoted management staff," says Brice Phillips. "We of the Phillips family thank all of our customers for their support and continued patronage. It will be our pleasure to serve our friends in Maryland and Virginia for years to come."

333 Waterside Drive   627-6600
Norfolk

CLAMS CASINO

24 top neck clams
   Garlic salt
   Lemon juice

   Seafood seasoning
⅔ cup fresh bread crumbs
4 slices bacon, cut into
   24 pieces

1. Shuck the clams, remove the top shell, and cut the clam away from the bottom shell.
2. Arrange the clams on a cookie sheet and sprinkle lightly with garlic salt, lemon juice, and seafood seasoning. Cover the clams with the bread crumbs and top each with 1 piece of bacon. Bake for 8-10 minutes at 425°.
3. Serve six clams per person on a bed of lettuce with melted butter to dip the clam in.

When selecting clams, be sure they are fresh and tightly closed and the saltier the better.

ONION SOUP GRATINÉE

2 *large onions, thinly sliced*
4 *tablespoons melted butter*
¼ *cup white wine*
4 *cans beef consommé*

Sherry (pale, dry), to taste
4 *slices toast, ½" cubed*
4 *slices Provolone cheese*
Parmesan cheese

1. Sauté the onions in butter until lightly brown.
2. Add the white wine and reduce the wine by half.
3. Add the consommé; bring to a boil. Remove from the heat and add the sherry.
4. Place the soup in individual stoneware soup crocks, sprinkle with croutons, and top with sliced Provolone. Sprinkle with Parmesan and brown under the broiler. Serve.

GARDEN SALAD WITH SWEET AND SOUR DRESSING

3 heads lettuce greens
Carrots, shredded
Onions, sliced
Celery, diced
Cucumbers, sliced

Green pepper, sliced
Radishes, sliced
Alfalfa sprouts
Tomatoes, sliced
SWEET AND SOUR
    DRESSING

Choose your favorite lettuce greens, wash, dry, and tear into bite-sized pieces. Mix with remaining vegetables, toss gently, and serve with Sweet and Sour Dressing.

SWEET AND SOUR DRESSING

¼ pound bacon
½ medium onion,
    finely chopped

2 cups white vinegar
1 cup sugar
Mayonnaise

1. Fry the bacon until crisp. Remove the bacon from the pan and drain. Reserve the bacon grease. Chop the bacon into fine pieces and set aside.
2. Sauté the onions in the bacon grease and set aside.
3. In a medium-sized pan, mix the vinegar and sugar and then bring to a boil. Add the bacon, sautéed onions, and drippings. While still hot, add mayonnaise until desired thickness is reached. Cool in the refrigerator.

The dressing ingredients provide a nice contrast in taste and an interesting prelude to the main course, especially to seafood.

SCALLOPS FLORENTINE

½ cup coarsely chopped
    onion
2 tablespoons butter
4 cups chopped spinach
4 tablespoons coarsely
    chopped parsley

¼ teaspoon garlic salt
    Dash of white pepper
½ cup fine bread crumbs
24 ounces scallops
12 ounces Virginia ham, sliced
    and cut into ½" strips

1. Sauté the onion in melted butter until transparent. Add the spinach, parsley, garlic salt, and white pepper. Sauté the spinach on medium heat for 5 minutes. Add the bread crumbs and mix well. Set aside to cool.

2. Clean and wash the scallops. Portion into four 6-ounce servings. Wrap each scallop with 1 strip of ham. In individual casserole dishes, layer the bottom with 4 ounces of spinach mixture and place the 6 ounce portion of scallops on top. Bake in a 400° oven for 15-20 minutes and serve.

Be sure to use sea scallops instead of bay scallops. Here, at Phillips, we use large (16-20 count) scallops fresh off the boat.

KEY LIME PIE

2 cups sweetened condensed milk (Eagle brand)

½ cup freshly squeezed lime juice

2 eggs

Pinch of salt

1 graham cracker pie shell

Whipped cream

Lime slices

Place the first four ingredients in a blender and mix well. Pour into an 8-inch pie shell and refrigerate for 3 hours. Garnish individual pieces with 1 tablespoon of fresh whipped cream and a slice of lime.

This is a nice light dessert to cap off a large dinner. There is a delightful contrast between the sweet crust and the tartness of the lime filling.

PHILLIPS WATERSIDE COFFEE

¾ ounce Bailey's Irish Creme

¾ ounce Myers' Rum

Coffee, fresh brewed

Whipped cream

Cherries

Nutmeg

For each serving, place the liqueurs in a cup, fill with coffee, and top with whipped cream. Garnish with a cherry and nutmeg.

SCALE O'DE WHALE

Dinner for Four

Champignon Supreme

Biscuit of Bisque

Salad with Poppy Seed Dressing

Trout Norfolk

Rum Cream Pie

Wine:

Pouilly Fuisse

Ronnie Bucher and Charles H. Sears, Jr., Proprietors

Robert C. Brooks, Chef

SCALE O'DE WHALE

The Scale O'de Whale is a dream come true for Ronnie Bucher and Charles H. Sears, Jr. Their joint effort transformed a snack bar-bait and tackle shop at the end of a 300-foot marina into an exclusive 200-seat seafood dining experience, featuring local and imported seafood dishes.

"We knew what we wanted to create in floor plan and decor but could not convey our ideas to an architect. We became our own designers and, taking the bull by the horns, ripped out walls, added on sections, and raised floors until we achieved our desired effect," explains Charlie Sears. Beams from barges grounded during the Civil War era were used to form the interior restaurant structure. The cyprus and juniper for the weathered wood walls came from barns one hundred years old. Decor is original nautical antiques, handmade tables, handmade high-backed booths, and live hanging plants in a pleasant, romantic atmosphere overlooking the marina vista.

Tables are set with pewter lanterns, china with white and blue Federal Eagle design, pistol handled flatware, red linen napkins, and menus rolled as a scroll. Wine menus are presented in handmade wooden hinged books.

"We are extremely pleased about written compliments on our decor, but even more pleased with outstanding reviews on our bill of fare," says Ronnie Bucher. "Our seafood is hand picked fresh daily, steaks are cut to order, salads are prepared individually and served with homemade dressings. We change menus often to preserve freshness and quality. Our dinners are served in consistently ample portions and attractively presented, to tantalize the palate of even the most discriminating gourmet."

3515 Shipwright Street   483-2772
Portsmouth

SCALE O' DE WHALE

CHAMPIGNON SUPREME

18 large, fresh mushrooms
½ pound butter, melted

CRAB STUFFING

1. Dry brush and remove the stems from the mushrooms.
2. Sauté the mushrooms lightly in butter until half-cooked.
3. Cool and stuff with the Crab Stuffing.
4. Place the stuffed mushrooms on a greased sheet. Brush lightly with drawn butter. Bake for 12 minutes at 350°, or until golden brown.

CRAB STUFFING

4 slices white bread, cubed
1 tablespoon diced pimentos
⅛ teaspoon hot sauce
¼ teaspoon Worchestershire sauce

¼ teaspoon Old Bay seasoning
3 tablespoons mayonnaise
1 pound Backfin crabmeat
   Parsley, for color

Mix all ingredients together until well blended.

This appetizer teases the palate. It is so excellent that it creates great anticipation for the courses that follow.

BISCUIT OF BISQUE

4 ounces shrimp, chunked
4 ounces scallops, chunked
4 ounces lobster, chunked
8 tablespoons butter
4 tablespoons flour
  Salt and pepper, to taste
1 medium onion, chopped
2 tablespoons parsley flakes
3 cups milk

1 cup canned bouillon
  or chicken broth
1 tablespoon cornstarch
¼ cup hot water
4 ounces Backfin crabmeat
4 ounces King crabmeat
½ cup cream or half & half
4 pastry shells
  Fresh parsley, for garnish

1. In a large pan, lightly sauté the shrimp, scallops, and lobster in 4 tablespoons butter until snow white. Set aside.
2. In a separate pan, melt the remaining butter. Stir in the flour, salt, and pepper. Add the onion and parsley flakes. Cook over low heat until the onion is almost done.
3. Slowly add the milk and then the bouillon to the onion mixture. Mix the cornstarch with the water and add to the bisque slowly, a little at a time.
4. Add the crabmeat and simmer 10 minutes.
5. Add the cream and simmer 10 minutes more. Thicken with more cornstarch if necessary.
6. Prepare the pastry shells as directed on the package.
7. Serve the bisque in the pastry shells. Garnish with fresh parsley.

The crabmeat is pre-cooked and does not need to be sautéed.

This bisque recipe was a favorite of Charlie Sears' mother. He improved it by adding a variety of the finest seafoods.

SALAD WITH POPPY SEED DRESSING

12 *medium-size spinach leaves*	1 *small head Iceberg lettuce*
1 *small head romaine lettuce*	4 *cucumber spears*
1 *small head Bibb lettuce*	4 *tomato wedges*
	POPPY SEED DRESSING

1. Rinse the spinach and lettuce leaves in cold water. Pat dry. Remove the stems from the spinach leaves. Tear equal amounts of spinach and lettuce into bite-size pieces.
2. Toss the spinach and lettuce greens together and then divide onto 4 chilled salad plates. Top each with a crisp cucumber spear and a tomato wedge. Serve with Poppy Seed Dressing.

POPPY SEED DRESSING

½ *cup vinegar*	¾ *teaspoon puréed onion*
¾ *cup sugar*	½ *teaspoon dry mustard*
1 *cup vegetable oil*	1½ *teaspoons poppy seeds*
	1 *teaspoon salt*

1. Heat the vinegar and sugar until the sugar is dissolved.
2. Mix the vinegar and sugar with all of the remaining ingredients. Chill before serving.

The Poppy Seed Dressing was created and perfected at Scale O'de Whale and is a favorite among the regular patrons.

TROUT NORFOLK

4 (1-1¼ pound) fresh, whole
   gray sea trout
   Seafood seasoning
3 large lemons
1 medium onion
1 stalk celery, cut into 4
   2" pieces
12 jumbo green shrimp
   (¾-1 pound total)

½ cup white table wine
   Vegetable oil for coating
⅓ cup melted butter
1 cup wild rice, uncooked
4 whole cherries
4 sprigs endive, for garnish
   (or other leafy green)

1. Starting 3 inches behind the gills, vertically cut the fish to the bones in 3 places, about 1½ inches apart. Make cuts 2½ inches long. Sprinkle seafood seasoning over the entire fish and rub it in.

2. Cut 24 paper-thin slices of lemon, plus eight equal wedges. Slice the onion into 4 equal wedges. Stuff the cavity of each fish with a wedge of lemon, onion, and a piece of celery. Place 2 lemon slices in each vertical cut, forming a V-shaped cradle for the shrimp (to be added later).

3. Cover the fish tail with aluminum foil (to prevent burning). Put the fish in a covered container and refrigerate 1 hour.

4. Peel and devein the shrimp, leaving on the tail. Put the shrimp in a glass container, cover with wine, and refrigerate 1 hour.

5. Preheat the oven to 375°.

6. Place the fish in a baking dish lightly coated with vegetable oil. Pour the melted butter over the fish and cook approximately 35 minutes, testing with a fork until it penetrates easily.

7. Meanwhile, prepare the wild rice according to package directions.

8. When the fish has about 5 minutes left to cook, remove it from the oven. Place 1 shrimp in each lemon cradle and fan the shrimp tails. Spoon the remainder of wine over the fish and return to the oven for 5 minutes.

9. Serve over a bed of wild rice. Skewer the remaining lemon wedges, cherries and endive on toothpicks for garnish. If desired, the trout may be accompanied by dill or tartar sauce.

While jogging one day along the back roads of Currituck, North Carolina, Charlie Sears created this recipe in his mind. It is a beautiful and popular entrée.

SCALE O'DE WHALE

RUM CREAM PIE

1 envelope gelatin	⅓ cup dark rum
½ cup cold water	1½ cups whipping cream
1 cup sugar	CRUMB CRUST
5 egg yolks	Unsweetened chocolate

1. Soften the gelatin in the cold water. Cook over low heat, almost to a boil, stirring to dissolve.
2. Beat the sugar and egg yolks until very light. Stir the gelatin into the egg mixture and cool.
3. Gradually add the rum, beating constantly.
4. Whip the cream in a separate bowl until it stands in soft peaks. Fold into the gelatin mixture. Cool until the mixture begins to set, then spoon into the Crumb Crust, and chill until firm. Garnish with grated chocolate.

CRUMB CRUST

2½ cups graham cracker crumbs	2 tablespoons sugar
½ cup butter, melted	½ teaspoon cinnamon

Combine ingredients and press into a 9-inch pie pan. Chill.

Rum Cream Pie is a Sears' family tradition.

Ships Cabin Seafood Restaurant

Dinner for Four

Oysters Bingo

Hydroponic Salad with Blue Cheese Dressing

Fresh Tuna en Papillote

Brie and Fresh Pineapple

Wines:

With Oysters Bingo—Charles Shaw Chardonnay, 1982

With Hydroponic Salad—Robert Pepi Sauvignon Blanc, 1982

With Fresh Tuna—Guenoc Chardonnay, 1981

With Brie and Fresh Pineapple—Robert Mondavi Moscato d'oro, 1982

Joseph Hoggard, Proprietor

Terry Marriott, Chef

SHIPS CABIN SEAFOOD RESTAURANT

When Joseph Hoggard was shopping for the ideal location for what was to become Norfolk's premiere seafood restaurant, he looked no further than his own backyard—the Ocean View section of Norfolk. True, it was a randy, wild, and largely run down section of town—not the kind of place one would expect to find anything remotely Continental. But Hoggard had done his homework. "I went to just about every famous seafood restaurant in the country, from New York to San Francisco, and the best ones are always in the most questionable neighborhoods. I came home to Ocean View and thought, 'Hell, this is great! I'm already here.'"

And so he is, with one of the finest dining establishments in the Hampton Roads area, and possibly the best seafood restaurant in Virginia. Hoggard's success is predicated on using just that kind of instinctual knowledge—the sense of using those resources at his disposal and turning the offbeat into the more-than-acceptable. His philosophy is homespun and simple: make the most of what you have, for you have more than you think. Quite so. The Chesapeake Bay-front location is an obvious advantage, and the proximity to fine, fresh Virginia seafood selections is nothing to sneeze at. Hoggard knows.

Fresh, fresh. Everything has to be straight from the deep blue and used immediately. As Hoggard sees it, there is no excuse *not* to, with everything—not with just those items from the briney deep. The salads are garden-fresh—hydroponic vegetables—locally-grown and delivered daily, roots still intact. "Now *that*," states Hoggard, "is *fresh*," as is the bread: cinnamon raisin, honey wheat, and blueberry, all baked daily in the kitchens, and special Ships Cabin manna to greet each diner.

Age has its place, too, and, where appropriate, it appears. There is aged Iowa beef that's cut to order in the kitchen, and the extensive wine list features California's best. Hoggard's annual trek through California's wine country sees to that. The wanderer, however, always returns to bring the spoils back home: to Norfolk, to Ocean View. The Ships Cabin—there's no place like it.

4110 East Ocean View Avenue   583-4659
Norfolk

OYSTERS BINGO

4 tablespoons butter
2 cups flour
24 fresh oysters,
   shells reserved
2 tablespoons white wine

2 tablespoons oyster juice
2 tablespoons
   minced shallots
1 tablespoon fresh
   chopped parsley
2 tablespoons lemon juice

1. Heat the butter in a large sauté pan.
2. Lightly flour the oysters and sauté until golden brown. Remove the oysters from the pan and place on heated shells.
3. Add 1 tablespoon flour to the pan to make a roux; add the wine, oyster juice, shallots, parsley, and lemon juice to the pan. Heat until the sauce thickens and pour over the oysters. Serve immediately.

The finest oysters in the world are found in the Chesapeake Bay and its tributaries. Everyone loves this recipe. Even people who say they don't like oysters find that they really do when they taste this preparation.

SHIPS CABIN SEAFOOD RESTAURANT

HYDROPONIC SALAD WITH BLUE CHEESE DRESSING

2   *heads lettuce*
2   *tomatoes*

8   *slices cucumber*
4   *large onion rings*
     BLUE CHEESE DRESSING

1. Gently tear the lettuce leaves from the root.
2. Arrange lettuce on four chilled plates; top each with a thick tomato slice, 2 slices of cucumber, and 1 onion ring.
3. Top with Blue Cheese Dressing.

SHIPS CABIN SEAFOOD RESTAURANT

BLUE CHEESE DRESSING

1 quart mayonnaise
1½ tablespoons white vinegar
½ cup buttermilk
1 tablespoon Worcestershire sauce

1½ teaspoons minced fresh garlic
½ teaspoon black pepper
12 ounces crumbled blue cheese

1. Stir all ingredients except the blue cheese in a large bowl by hand until blended.
2. Beat on medium speed of the mixer until smooth.
3. Fold in the blue cheese and allow the flavor to mellow for several hours.

Probably 80% of the salads ordered in our restaurant have this dressing by request. It goes very well with seafood and with wine. The flavor of the cheese comes through and yet doesn't offend the wine palate.

FRESH TUNA EN PAPILLOTE

Parchment paper
4 tablespoons
   melted butter
8 medium asparagus spears

4 (10 ounce) fillets of tuna
1 teaspoon tarragon
   Kosher salt and white
   pepper to taste

1. Preheat the oven to 350°. Cut 4 circles of parchment paper 14-16" in diameter. Butter one side of each circle. Criss-cross the center of each circle with 2 asparagus spears.
2. Sprinkle each side of the tuna with tarragon, salt, and pepper. Place over the asparagus spears. Dot the fish with the remaining butter. Fold the parchment paper over and crimp the edges to seal.
3. Bake until the parchment has puffed, about 12-14 minutes. Serve immediately and allow the guests to break open the parchment paper.

Tuna is found fresh locally in the spring, summer, and fall. When cooked in parchment paper, the moisture is retained in the fish. When the parchment is opened, the fragrance bursts into the air.

BRIE AND FRESH PINEAPPLE

1 pineapple   ¼ wheel brie

1. Remove the pineapple from its shell. Core and slice into ¼″ sections.
2. Slice the brie and arrange with pineapple slices on a clear glass plate.

This light dessert is very cleansing and really finishes off a meal. With Moscato d'oro wine, it is really a wonderful combination and a delightful way to end the evening.

Dinner for Six

Shrimp Citron

Radiatore in Cream with Smoked Salmon and Caviar

Caesar Salad

*Noisettes of Lamb Dijonnaise
with Black Truffles*

Asparagus with Lemon Butter

Poached Meringues with Blueberry Sauce

Wines:

Chateau Smith Haut Lafite, Blanc 1981

Chateau de la Chaize, 1982

Monroe Duncan, Proprietor and Chef

Tony Klementzos, Proprietor

SUDDENLY LAST SUMMER

Like its eclectic name, Suddenly Last Summer remains one of the Norfolk area's most unique restaurants. "Chefateur" Monroe Duncan and his associate, Tony Klementzos, conceived the idea for "Suddenly" (as it is known to its local habitués) in 1979. Deliberately small and personal, the restaurant's decor is often lightly referred to as "nouvelle Florida" because of its flamingo and aquatic motif mural that dominates a full wall of the interior. Some of the same design has been incorporated as an exterior fresco on the building. Hanging plants, a random gathering of objets d'art, interior shutters, and subdued lighting complete the summery atmosphere.

One of the distinguishing features of Suddenly Last Summer is the presence of the chef in an "exposed" kitchen which looks out on the dining room and the miniscule bar. From behind a wide counter, Chef Duncan communicates with his knowledgeable patrons who swear they would follow him no matter where his restaurant might be located in the Tidewater area. "We have kept away from a ponderous, too-formal atmosphere in spite of the fact that we look on the menu as a serious representation of dishes from a wide variety of international origins. Dining at Suddenly is fun as well as a culinary experience," the chef says.

In its colorful, theatrical aura (which is why the name of Tennessee Williams' famous play so aptly fits Suddenly Last Summer), the dining experience is intimate. Duncan and Klementzos obtained a store front ice cream parlor in the Ocean View area of Norfolk for their unique restaurant and cleverly adapted it to its present theme. "We wanted to present a creative concept in restauranting, not one restricted to pre-conceived ideas and predictable menus," Klementzos says.

On a nightly basis and at lunch, the restaurant features unusual and individual preparations. It might be something in a remarkable pasta or one of the imaginative seafood creations for which Chef Duncan has a special affinity. "Norfolk has a number of very well-known seafood dishes that are indigenous to the area," Duncan says, "and we often feature them in preparations that center on the original ideas rather than on the variations that have been done on them over the years."

About the purpose of Suddenly Last Summer, Chef Duncan says, "We intend our food to make definite statements about cooking as an art. Our approach is always classical—our results always brand new."

9225 Granby Street   587-0077
Norfolk

SHRIMP CITRON

½ pound lightly salted butter
2 teaspoons chopped shallots
1 tablespoon chopped parsley
1 tablespoon orange zest
24 (15/20 count) green shrimp,
    peeled and deveined

6 tablespoons orange juice
Salt and pepper, to taste
Watercress, for garnish
Orange slices, for garnish

1. In a sauté pan, melt the butter. Add the shallots, parsley, and orange zest to the butter. Sauté briefly, until the shallots appear cellophane, then add the shrimp, orange juice, salt, and pepper. Cover the sauté pan and allow to cook over high heat until the shrimp are done without overcooking.

2. Serve at once. If the liaison between the butter and orange juice breaks, add more orange juice to reconstitute. Garnish with watercress and thin slices of orange.

Simplicity is the key in cooking. The simpler the method, the better the outcome.

RADIATORE IN CREAM
WITH SMOKED SALMON AND CAVIAR

4 cups radiatore noodles
  Dash of salt and olive oil
½ pound lightly salted butter
2 cups heavy whipping cream

6 ounces smoked salmon,
  sliced
2 ounces red salmon caviar
  Pepper, to taste

1. Thrust the radiatore noodles into boiling water with salt and olive oil. Allow to boil until *al dente*—barely tender, remove from water,
1. and immediately wash in a sieve with cold water until the noodles are chilled. Set aside, tossing them in a touch of olive oil to keep them from sticking together.
2. Melt the butter in a saucepan and add the cream. Bring the cream and butter to a boil and reduce the liquid until it thickens. Add the salmon and caviar. Boil and reduce for a few minutes until the salmon turns pink and the sauce is thickened.
3. Quickly reheat the noodles in boiling water and drain them. Put the hot noodles into the sauce and toss. Serve immediately.

Radiatore noodles have little pockets like radiators which hold the sauce. When you take a bite of this pasta, there is an explosion of flavor.

CAESAR SALAD

18 large croutons
 1 large clove garlic, peeled
   Freshly ground pepper
12 anchovy fillets
 ¾ cup olive oil
 ¼ cup wine vinegar
 2 dashes Worcestershire
   sauce (Lea & Perrins)

 1 teaspoon dry mustard
   (Coleman's)
 1 coddled egg
   Juice of 1 lemon
 3 heads romaine lettuce
3-4 tablespoons grated
   Parmesan cheese

1. Prepare the croutons by sautéing large cubes of bread in butter until brown. Set aside.
2. Into a Brazilian Rosewood salad bowl (or Ash, Elm, etc.), crush the clove of garlic forcing the oil into the wood. Remove the excess shreds of garlic and then grind the pepper into the bowl. Add the anchovies and crush them into a paste. If the anchovies resist too much, add a touch of vinegar to dissolve them. Add the oil and vinegar and blend thoroughly. Add the Worcestershire, dry mustard, and coddled egg. Blend until the dressing becomes a creamy liaison, then add the lemon juice.
3. Prepare the romaine by separating the leaves from the stalk, washing, drying, and chilling them until they are crisp.
4. Toss the leaves into the dressing with the croutons. Sprinkle the top of the lettuce with Parmesan cheese until the leaves resemble the first snow fall. Toss the entire mixture no more than 21 turns (otherwise the lettuce becomes bruised) and serve on chilled plates.

This is perhaps the most controversial salad tossed around the world. The origin of this salad is Mexico, although California claims it. We have further modified and improved it, as you will see.

NOISETTES of LAMB DIJONNAISE
with BLACK TRUFFLES

3 *loins of lamb*
3 *whole black truffles*

DIJONNAISE SAUCE
Watercress, for garnish

1. Grill the loins to the color desired.
2. Slice the loins into medallions; there should be 3 or 4 medallions per person.
3. Slice the truffles and sauté in butter just before serving.
4. On a rather warm dinner plate, ladle 5 ounces of Dijonnaise Sauce. Arrange the sliced lamb loin on top of the sauce. Aesthetically arrange the truffles atop the lamb medallions. Garnish with a large sprig of watercress and serve.

DIJONNAISE SAUCE

2 *teaspoons finely chopped*
   shallots
1 *tablespoon clarified butter*

3 *tablespoons Poupon*
   Dijon mustard
4 *cups DEMI-GLACE*
½ *cup heavy whipping cream*

1. In a saucepan, sauté the shallots in butter until transparent, adding the mustard and Demi-glace. Whisk the mixture until completely blended.
2. Add the cream and whisk again, until the mixture is completely blended.

SUDDENLY LAST SUMMER

DEMI-GLACE

5 ounces salted pork
1 large onion, diced
4 large carrots, diced
1 tablespoon thyme
½ cup roux (equal parts flour and butter)

2 quarts chicken and beef stocks, mixed
2 cups white wine
4 tablespoons tomato paste
1 cup Madeira

1. Render the salted pork.
2. Into the grease from the pork, sauté the onion and carrot with the thyme until the vegetables begin to brown. Add the roux and mix thoroughly with the vegetables, allowing it to brown a little, but being careful not to burn the mixture at this point. Add the stocks and white wine. Mix the roux into the stocks completely and allow the combination to boil, remaining alert so that the sauce does not scorch or burn. As the sauce thickens, add the tomato paste and additional stock if the sauce is too thick. The consistency must be just so.
3. After the sauce has thickened and has browned nicely, remove it from the heat and strain through a seive and cheesecloth for a very clean sauce.
4. Add the Madeira and reduce by one-fourth until the proper viscosity is achieved.

This dish is a highlight of our Christmas Grande Fête Gastronomique. Its preparation is a bit complex, but its presentation is absolutely gorgeous!

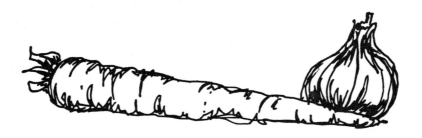

ASPARAGUS WITH LEMON BUTTER

24-36 stalks of fresh asparagus
1½ cups butter

1½ teaspoons lemon juice
Salt and pepper, to taste

1. Remove the tough ends from stalks of asparagus, then blanch the stalks in boiling water for 1 minute. From each stalk cut off a 1-inch section and chop up finely. Set aside.
2. When ready to serve the entrée, sauté the asparagus stalks and chopped asparagus in butter and add a touch of lemon juice, salt, and pepper. Serve with chopped portion atop the asparagus stalks.

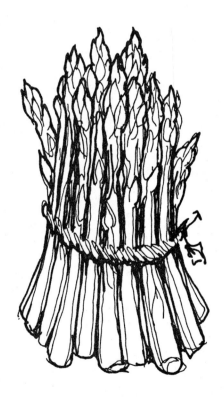

POACHED MERINGUES WITH BLUEBERRY SAUCE

8 egg whites
3½ cups granulated sugar

Milk, for poaching
2 pints fresh blueberries
½ cup Crème de Cassis

1. Separate the eggs, retaining the egg whites, being careful not to touch the whites, and place them in a very clean mixing bowl. Whip them by hand or with an electric mixer until they stand in peaks.
2. Continue to whip, adding 1½ cups granulated sugar very slowly in a thin stream until the whites appear glazed.
3. In a large pan heat the milk to "shimmering" temperature. With a spoon form the meringue into large egg-shaped pieces and poach them in the milk 5 minutes on each side, turning them once. Set aside.
4. Purée the blueberries in a blender, adding the Cassis and 2 cups of sugar, blending each into the sauce. Heat this sauce until it steams. Pour the hot blueberry sauce onto the dessert plate and place the meringue in it, then pour a little more sauce on top of the meringue.

This dessert is light as air—clouds of sweetness.

THE TRELLIS

Dinner for Four

Chesapeake Oysters and Shiitake
Mushrooms Served in Warm Brioche

Salad of Chicory, Beets, and Walnuts
with Mustard Vinaigrette

Sautéed Urbanna Duck Breasts
with Apples and Roasted Chestnuts on Hazelnut Fettuccine

Chocolate Walnut Torte

Wines:
With Oysters—Sterling Sauvignon Blanc, 1982
With Duck—Stags Leap Gamay Beaujolais, 1981
With Torte—Schramsberg Cuvee de Pinot, Napa 1979

John Curtis and Tom Power, Proprietors
Marcel Desaulniers, Proprietor and Executive Chef
Philip Delaplane, Assistant Chef
Jeff Duncan, Assistant Chef
Andrew O'Connell, Pastry Chef

THE TRELLIS

Recognized by *The New York Times, The Washington Post,* and *Food and Wine Magazine* as one of the finest restaurants in Virginia, The Trellis, with its country and French antiques, rare prints, California Grill Room, florally inspired Garden Room, and verdant Trellis Room offers a seasonal American menu that can only be called inspirational. The Trellis opened in the fall of 1980, the happy result of a partnership of three friends whose quest for the innovative use of local fresh products and seafood ultimately translated into its founding.

The seasonal offerings keep regular patrons on their toes as it takes many visits to sample one's way through the eclectic menu. Each season's selection takes full advantage of Virginia's bountiful harvest of fresh produce and herbs, poultry, game, and seafood. Chef and partner Marcel Desaulniers, a slender athletic man of French Canadian heritage, belies the cliché that all good chefs must be fat. Whether it is the development of a new game recipe to be cooked on the mesquite-fired grill or one of his devastating chocolate desserts, such as his recent "Death by Chocolate," Marcel's fine touch is apparent everywhere.

Joined by Tom Power, a noted authority on wine and cheese, and John Curtis, a businessman whose wine knowledge is encyclopedic, the three men take great pleasure in the painstaking day-to-day decisions which distinguish a great restaurant from a very good one.

Duke of Gloucester Street   229-8610
Williamsburg

CHESAPEAKE OYSTERS AND SHIITAKE MUSHROOMS SERVED IN WARM BRIOCHE

2 pints heavy cream
2 ounces sliced shiitake
   mushrooms
4 teaspoons dry white wine

2 teaspoons chopped shallots
4 cups Chesapeake oysters
   Salt and pepper, to taste
4 BRIOCHE,
   hollowed and warm

1. Pour the heavy cream into a heavy sauce pot. Place the pot on the stove top and adjust the heat so that the cream will simmer slowly. Allow the cream to reduce in volume by half of the original amount.
2. Cook the shiitake mushrooms with white wine and shallots for 10 minutes. Add the oysters and cook only until the oysters begin to curl around the edges.
3. Add the reduced cream to the oysters and mushrooms and season with salt and pepper. Divide the hot mixture equally into each warm Brioche and serve.

This recipe provides a very unusual combination: regional and classical cuisine are combined resulting in an elegant presentation.

BRIOCHE

4½ cups sifted all purpose flour
2 teaspoons salt
2 tablespoons granulated sugar
½ cup warm water

1¾ tablespoons granulated yeast
7 large eggs
1½ cups unsalted butter, softened

1. Sift the flour and salt together; set aside. Dissolve the sugar in warm water in a large mixing bowl. Add the yeast and dissolve by stirring slowly.
2. Place the flour and salt on top of the sugar and yeast mixture. Then add 6 eggs on top of the flour mixture. Mix slowly until all ingredients are combined.
3. Stir the mixture for several minutes until the dough becomes smooth and elastic, then add the softened butter 2 tablespoons at a time until all the butter is completely incorporated.
4. Cover and bench proof the dough until double in volume.
5. Punch down the dough and proof in the refrigerator until the dough is firm and workable.
6. Measure 3-ounce pats of dough.
7. Brush oven-proof coffee cups with softened butter.
8. Pinch a marble-sized piece of dough from each pat and reserve.
9. Form each pat of dough into a round shape and place in a buttered cup.
10. Form each marble-sized piece of dough into a pear shape.
11. Make a dent in the round dough and place a pear piece into dent after wetting the pointed end in water.
12. Proof the dough until double in size.
13. Beat the remaining egg with 1 tablespoon water. Brush the egg wash over the dough.
14. Bake at 350° for 15-18 minutes.

SALAD OF CHICORY, BEETS, AND WALNUTS, WITH MUSTARD VINAIGRETTE

6 medium-size beets
2 full heads chicory
    (curly endive)
8 ounces walnuts
2 teaspoons Dijon mustard

1 teaspoon Pommery mustard
2 teaspoons chopped tarragon
½ teaspoon minced garlic
    Salt and pepper
¼ cup white wine vinegar
¾ cup olive oil

1. Cook, peel, and slice the beets. Hold under refrigeration.
2. Thoroughly wash the chicory and break apart into 2-inch segments. Pat dry and refrigerate.
3. Toast the walnuts for 10 minutes in a 350° oven. Allow to cool, then break up into smaller pieces. Reserve.
4. In a mixing bowl, place the mustards, tarragon, garlic, salt, and pepper. Whisk in the vinegar combining all ingredients thoroughly. Slowly whisk in the olive oil. Adjust taste with additional salt and pepper if necessary.
5. For service, arrange slices of beets close to the outside edge of 9-inch dinner plates. Place chicory on the plates in the center. Sprinkle dressing over the chicory. Finish by garnishing with toasted walnuts.

It is best to buy and then cook beets with "tops" on because then the beets retain their color intensity and flavor.

This is a colorful, seasonal salad to serve in the summer and fall.

SAUTÉED URBANNA DUCK BREASTS
WITH APPLES AND ROASTED CHESTNUTS
ON HAZELNUT FETTUCCINE

4   (4½-5 pound) fresh ducks
    Salt and pepper, to taste
1   quart dry red wine
4   teaspoons cooking oil
4   teaspoons butter
8   teaspoons chopped shallots

4   golden delicious apples,
    peeled and sliced
24 whole chestnuts, roasted,
    peeled and sliced
1½ cups heavy cream
24 ounces (dry weight)
    HAZELNUT FETTUCCINE
½   cup softened butter

1. Remove the duck breast from each duck carcass. Place the skinless breast between a folded sheet of aluminum foil and flatten the breast with a meat cleaver. Season with salt and pepper.

2. Marinate the duck breasts in red wine for 25-30 minutes. Remove the duck breasts from the marinade and refrigerate until you are ready to cook them.

3. Heat the cooking oil and butter in a sauté pan. When very hot, brown the duck breasts on both sides. Place the browned duck breasts in a 350° oven just until the pasta is done, for 3-6 minutes.

4. Remove most of the cooking oil and butter mixture from the pan. Add the chopped shallots and sauté for 2-3 minutes.

5. Add the sliced apples and sliced chestnuts to the pan and cook for 3-4 minutes. Add the heavy cream and allow to simmer with other ingredients for 2-3 minutes. While this is simmering, cook the pasta in boiling salted water for 3-4 minutes.

6. Remove the pasta from the water, drain thoroughly, and toss with softened butter. Place the pasta in a serving dish, remove the duck breasts from the oven, and then place on the pasta. Finish with sauce.

Save the marinade and use with the duck legs for a separate meal. Duck legs should be marinated for 48 hours then grilled over a charcoal or wood fire.

HAZELNUT FETTUCCINE

1½ cups ground hazelnuts (filberts)
5 cups all purpose flour

4 tablespoons water
2 teaspoons salt
2 tablespoons oil
4 large eggs

1. Combine the hazelnuts and flour in a mixing bowl.
2. In a separate bowl, mix the water, salt, oil, and eggs together.
3. Knead the egg mixture into the hazelnut and flour mixture. Continue to knead until the dough forms a ball.
4. Remove the dough from the bowl and knead by hand until soft.
5. Cover the dough and allow it to relax for 1 hour under refrigeration.
6. Roll and cut the dough into the desired pasta shape.

Cut pasta may be tossed with cornmeal and held under refrigeration for 2 days. Before cooking, gently toss the pasta to remove the excess cornmeal.

The key to this whole dish is getting fresh ducks; therefore, it is a seasonal entrée served in the fall and winter.

CHOCOLATE WALNUT TORTE

1 *cup granulated sugar*
5 *ounces semi-sweet chocolate, cut into small pieces*
6 *tablespoons unsalted butter, softened*
8 *eggs, separated*

2 *cups coarsely ground walnuts*
2 *tablespoons fresh bread crumbs*
Pinch of salt
MOCHA BUTTERCREAM
Walnut halves, for garnish

1. Preheat the oven to 375°. Butter a 10-inch round, 2½-inch deep spring-form pan. Line it with a round of waxed paper. Butter and flour the paper and sides of the pan. Tap out the excess.
2. In a saucepan, combine the sugar with ¼ cup of water and cook over moderate heat, stirring occasionally, until the sugar dissolves, about 5 minutes.
3. Add the chocolate, remove from heat, and stir until the chocolate is melted. Allow to cool 15 minutes.
4. In a medium bowl, beat the butter until it is light. Beat in the egg yolks one at a time, beating until each is incorporated before adding another. On low speed, add half the chocolate syrup, then 1¾ cups of the ground walnuts, then the remaining syrup and the bread crumbs, mixing just enough to blend after each addition.
5. In a large bowl, beat the egg whites with the salt until stiff peaks form. Stir ⅓ of the egg whites into the chocolate mixture to lighten it, then pour the chocolate mixture into the egg whites, 'etting it run down one side of the bowl. Gently fold the two together until thoroughly blended. Gently pour into the prepared pan and bake in the center of the oven for 35-40 minutes or until the center feels set when pressed.
6. Remove the torte from the oven and allow to cool in the pan for 15 minutes. Release the sides and invert onto a rack covered with a paper towel. Remove the pan bottom and waxed paper. Let the torte cool completely, for at least 2 hours, before frosting.
7. Split the cake in half and place the top side down on a platter. Cover the cake with Mocha Buttercream. Place the second layer on top of the first, smooth side up; frost the top and the sides of the cake. Reserve 1 cup of Mocha Buttercream for decoration.

8. Press the remaining ground nuts into the sides of the cake. Using a pastry bag fitted with a star tip, decorate the top edges of the cake and then press the walnut halves into the stars.

MOCHA BUTTERCREAM

6 ounces semi-sweet chocolate, cut into small pieces

⅓ cup water

2 teaspoons instant espresso powder

5 ounces unsalted butter, softened

3 egg yolks

⅔ cup confectioners sugar

1. In a heavy saucepan, combine the chocolate, water, and espresso powder. Stir over low heat until the chocolate is melted and then cool completely.
2. Cream the butter until light, then beat in the egg yolks one at a time, and add the confectioners sugar. Beat in the chocolate mixture, blending thoroughly.

This dessert has a beautiful appearance and is surprisingly light to eat. We often use fresh fruit bread (prune, apricot, or apple) for the bread crumbs—this gives a wonderful flavor and texture to the torte.

Dinner for Four

Oyster and Spinach Bisque

Watercress topped with a Blue Cheese Vinaigrette

Chateau Wesley

Wesley's Peanut Butter Cheesecake

Wines:

With Oyster and Spinach Bisque—Chardonnay, Far Niente

With Chateau Wesley—Cabernet Sauvignon, Jordan

After Dinner-—Edelwein, Freemark Abbey

*Wesley Hull, Karen Hull, Jim Graziadei
and Bob Lynch, Proprietors
Jim Graziadei, Chef*

Wesley's was founded in 1980 by Wesley Hull, his wife, Karen, and Jim Graziadei. This restaurant was started under the basic premise that nothing would ever be compromised, a restaurant where people can count on receiving a consistently fine meal, professionally served, without being pretentious.

Although Wesley opened a second restaurant in Greenwich, Connecticut, in 1983, the traditions and philosophies continue to be carried on by Jim Graziadei and Bob Lynch. Jim, the chef/partner since the inception, has a lengthy food background and prepares the finest in American Continental cuisine. Bob, only recently becoming maitre d'/partner, has spent several years in the capacity of waiter and has a thorough understanding of what is required to deliver the type of service that Wesley's demands.

Another tradition of Wesley's is the very extensive wine list that is offered to their patrons. Currently, there are in excess of 220 wines for diners to select among. Every quality wine producing region from Europe and America is represented, and Wesley is noted for his conservative pricing policy.

Even though Wesley's enjoys a national reputation, it is a local favorite. It best qualifies to be described as a destination restaurant. A destination restaurant is defined as being out of the way and hard to find. Virginia Beach and Tidewater residents know that they can travel to Wesley's via the back roads and never have to traverse the congested resort area.

Wesley's is noted for its originality in food. The staff goes to extremes personalizing everything they serve; for example, they make their own breads, butters, salad dressings, sauces, and desserts. All of these change regularly. This is part of what makes Wesley's an exciting dining experience and keeps people coming back over and over again.

500 Pinewood Drive   422-1511
Virginia Beach

OYSTER AND SPINACH BISQUE

¼ cup butter
1 medium onion, puréed
2 large cloves garlic, puréed
1 pint oysters
⅙ cup flour
2 cups heavy cream

5 ounces frozen chopped spinach or fresh spinach, chopped
1 tablespoon chicken base or 2 bouillon cubes dissolved in ¼ cup water
Salt and white pepper

1. Melt half of the butter in a large pot. Sauté the puréed onion and garlic in the butter. Add the oysters and sauté them until the edges curl.
2. While the oysters are cooking, melt the remaining butter in a pan and stir in the flour to make a *roux*. Stir constantly until smooth.
3. Add the roux to the onion and oysters. When the mixture begins to boil, add the cream, spinach, and chicken base. Cook until the spinach is done but do not let it boil. Stir constantly. Add salt and pepper to taste.

This bisque is by far the most popular soup served at Wesley's. It has received so many raves and is so often requested that it is now a permanent part of the menu while other soup selections change daily.

WATERCRESS TOPPED WITH A BLUE CHEESE VINAIGRETTE

2 bunches fresh watercress
¼ cup chopped walnuts

¼ cup cooked bacon, crumbled

1. Trim off the bottom edge of each bunch of watercress. Wash thoroughly and allow to air dry.
2. Arrange watercress neatly on four chilled salad plates and top with the Blue Cheese Vinaigrette. Sprinkle each salad with 1 tablespoon chopped walnuts and 1 tablespoon crumbled bacon.

BLUE CHEESE VINAIGRETTE

¼ cup red wine vinegar
¾ cup 80/20 oil (80%
   vegetable oil and 20%
   olive oil

¼ teaspoon salt
¼ teaspoon white pepper
½ cup crumbled blue cheese

Blend with a wire whisk the red wine vinegar, oil, salt, and pepper. Then add the crumbled blue cheese and stir lightly with a spoon. Keep refrigerated until ready to serve. Stir gently before serving.

This salad offers an incredible blend of flavors that nicely offset the sometimes bitterness of the watercress.

CHATEAU WESLEY

1 section beef tenderloin
  (36-48 ounces net after
  side strap and silver skin
  have been removed)
2 bottles flat beer
1 cup 80/20 oil (80% vegetable
  oil and 20% olive oil)

4 ounces lemon juice
6 large garlic cloves, pressed
2 tablespoons sugar
1½ teaspoons salt
6 whole cloves
2 tablespoons Dijon mustard
  Béarnaise Sauce
  (see index)

1. Peel, or have the butcher peel, the tenderloin, removing the side strap and silver skin.
2. Flatten the beer; mix with oil.
3. In a blender, mix the lemon juice, garlic, sugar, salt, cloves, and mustard for 3 minutes. Add this mixture to the beer and oil.
4. Marinate the tenderloin for a minimum of 48 hours.
5. Remove from the marinade and charbroil to medium rare. Serve sliced and top with Béarnaise Sauce.

This is a perfect recipe to use for summer entertaining.

WESLEY'S PEANUT BUTTER CHEESECAKE

CRUST:
- 6 ounces vanilla wafers
- 2 tablespoons melted butter
- ½ cup sugar

TOPPING:
- 1 cup sour cream
- ½ cup sugar
- 4 ounces melted semi-sweet chocolate chips

CHEESE FILLING:
- 1½ pounds cream cheese
- 4 eggs
- 1½ cups sugar
- 6 ounces peanut butter
- 4-6 ounces semi-sweet chocolate chips

1. *CRUST:* In a food processor or Cuisinart, blend all Crust ingredients until smooth. Then border around an 8½ or 9" spring-form pan and bottom, pressing firmly.
2. *CHEESE FILLING:* Blend all Filling ingredients except the chocolate chips in a processor or Cuisinart until smooth. When all ingredients are smooth, add the chocolate chips and blend for 10 seconds. Pour into the prepared crust. Bake approximately 1½ hours at 350° or until the center is firm.
3. *TOPPING:* Blend all Topping ingredients in a processor or Cuisinart until smooth and hold until the cake is out of the oven. When the cheesecake comes out of the oven, allow approximately 15 minutes to settle. Then cover with Topping and bake for exactly 10 minutes. Remove and cool in the refrigerator for a minimum of 3 hours before serving.

Biting into a piece of this delectable dessert is quite like biting into a Reese's Peanut Butter Cup. This is our most popular cheesecake and the recipe is often requested.

Yorgy's restaurant

Dinner for Six

Oysters Chesapeake

Red Bean Soup

Asparagus Oriental

Lamb en Pastry

Pears Yorgy

Wines:

With Oysters—Stag's Leap Chardonnay

With Soup—Sterling Sauvignon Blanc

With Lamb—Chateau Montelena Cabernet Sauvignon

Chuck Mamoudis, Proprietor and Chef

YORGY'S

When billionaire Armand Hammer came to Tidewater recently and wanted to have dinner with a small group of friends, he chose Yorgy's, an intimate eatery a block off the oceanfront in Virginia Beach, because of its reputation for excellent food and an exciting, creative menu. "He said I had real talent and that if I were in Los Angeles I'd have customers standing in line to get in," says chef-owner Chuck Mamoudis, with a proud grin, as he watches Virginia Beach's locals file into Yorgy's.

In the three years Mamoudis and his wife, Debra, have operated Yorgy's (a Greek nickname for Mamoudis' middle name, George), it has quickly become one of the area's premier eating establishments.

From the lavender Italian tile tables set with sparkling crystal and elegantly-flowered china to the cane chairs and hanging greenery, Yorgy's has a feeling of casual elegance. "We wanted to do away with the austere, formal feeling of some top-quality restaurants, so we opened the kitchen to view from the dining room," Mamoudis explains. That allows customers to talk with the chef and brings Mamoudis out into the dining room to mingle.

The menus, which change weekly, are eclectic, drawing on Mamoudis' Greek heritage, Virginia up-bringing, Creole exposure during college, extensive culinary reading, and constant experimentation. Each evening features three appetizers, three salads, a soup, seven entrées, and a choice of four to six desserts, all prepared by Mamoudis. The offerings are nothing short of a United Nations gastronomic gathering—Chicken Florentine, Creole Country Paté, Lamb Chops Nicoise, Beef Scappati, Wiener Schnitzel, Garrides Mia Feta, Lamb à la Hydra, Escargot in Wonton, and Italian Chicken Breasts.

"People tell us they've never tasted so much flavor in food before," Mamoudis says, "and they can't imagine there are so many different items on the menu or that it changes each week."

To Mamoudis, a chef is an individual who understands flavorings and who knows how to incorporate them into a tasty and unusual dish. "That creates spontaneity, an ability to be creative, to reach as far as you can. That's what I love about food: it's as unlimited as your imagination."

214 40th Street   422-1586
Virginia Beach

OYSTERS CHESAPEAKE

36 oysters, shucked in
   the shell
 1 *cup fresh grated horseradish*

3 *whole lemons, quartered*
  Salt and ground black
  pepper

1. Lift the oysters from the bottom of the shell.
2. Place a pinch of horseradish along the bottom of the shell and replace the oysters.
3. Squeeze fresh lemon juice over the oysters and season with salt and ground black pepper.

The brilliance of the horseradish enhances the flavor of the chilled oysters.

RED BEAN SOUP

2 cups red kidney beans	3 cloves garlic, finely minced
¼ cup butter	Salt and pepper, to taste
½ pound ham, chopped	1 tablespoon Worchestershire sauce
½ pound sausage (Italian or Polish)	1 bay leaf
1 medium onion, finely chopped	1 tablespoon thyme
1 medium green pepper, finely chopped	1 teaspoon cayenne pepper
2 ribs celery, finely chopped	1 cup whole peeled tomatoes

1. Soak the beans overnight in 1 quart of water.
2. In a large pot, melt the butter over medium heat. Add the ham and sausage and sauté. Set aside the ham and sausage, reserving the drippings.
3. To the drippings, add the onion, green pepper, celery, and garlic and sauté for 5 minutes. Add the seasonings and sauté for 2 minutes more.
4. Next, add the whole peeled tomatoes. After incorporated, add 2 quarts of water and the beans. Simmer for 1½-2 hours or until the mixture has reduced by half. Adjust seasoning with salt and pepper.

My years of living in Louisiana helped me create this hearty winter soup. It is just the right thing to serve on a cold, crisp night.

ASPARAGUS ORIENTAL

2 tablespoons olive oil	Romaine lettuce
¼ cup cider vinegar	1½ pounds fresh asparagus, parboiled and chilled
¼ cup Teriyaki sauce	
2 tablespoons honey	1 cup sliced toasted almonds

1. Place the first 4 ingredients in a bowl and mix well.
2. Line the bottom of six salad plates with lettuce and divide the asparagus among the plates.
3. Mix the dressing and pour it over the salad. Garnish with a sprinkle of almonds.

There are no bland dishes served in this restaurant. This asparagus salad has an unusual sweet and sour flavor which really gets the taste buds working.

LAMB EN PASTRY

1½ racks of lamb	1 pound Phyllo pastry
½ cup olive oil	Butter
Salt and pepper, to taste	GREEK EGG LEMON SAUCE

1. Cut the lamb loins from the rack and then cut the loin in half. Rub each lamb portion with olive oil and lightly salt and pepper.
2. Wrap each loin with 4 sheets of pastry, buttering each layer.
3. Place on a baking sheet and bake 15-20 minutes at 400°.
4. Remove the lamb from the oven and place on a serving plate. Garnish the plate with in-season vegetables and glaze the lamb with the Greek Egg Lemon Sauce.

GREEK EGG LEMON SAUCE

1 pint heavy cream	4 egg yolks
½ cup rich chicken stock	½ tablespoon cornstarch
Juice of 3 lemons	Salt and pepper, to taste

1. Place the cream and chicken stock in a saucepan over medium high heat. Bring slightly to a boil.
2. Add the lemon juice to the egg yolks and slowly add to the mixture. Incorporate thoroughly.
3. Mix the cornstarch with ¼ cup water and add to the sauce, a little at a time, until the desired consistency is reached. Adjust seasoning with salt and pepper.

While this lamb dish is not difficult to prepare, it is quite elegant and impressive.

PEARS YORGY

6 *pears with stems*	1 *cup orange marmalade*
3 *cups water*	4 *tablespoons Grand Marnier*
¾ *cup sugar*	½ *gallon French vanilla*
4 *tablespoons lemon juice*	*ice cream*

1. Pare and core the pears, leaving stems intact.
2. Place the pears, water, sugar, and lemon juice in a Dutch oven on high heat for 5 minutes and then turn the heat down to low for 20 minutes.
3. Remove the pears and simmer the liquid until 1½ cups remain. Add the marmalade and Grand Marnier and remove from the heat.
4. Place each pear upright, stem up. Generously glaze with sauce. Garnish with 3 miniature scoops of ice cream and chill.

The marmalade makes this recipe unusual. This is a real favorite because it is light and refreshing after a meal of many courses.

Polly and Tom Chisman

From their Georgian home on the north shore of Hampton Roads, Polly and Tom Chisman have an exceptional opportunity to appreciate the majesty of this great harbor. On its beautiful and historic waters, the first Americans came to Jamestown in 1607, and today the largest ships in the world are daily visitors—viewed with a deep sense of belonging to both the past and the future.

Polly and Tom met in high school (he says she had pretty legs and a "punkin" face). She went to Hollins; he, to the University of Virginia. Today they have four children, twelve grandchildren, a dog, and a continuing zest for family, friends, travel, and good food.

Tom's family came to Virginia in 1621, and Polly is a descendant of the Michie family of Albemarle County. He is in his 37th year as a broadcast station executive. He used to sail and scuba dive before heart attacks and open heart surgery slowed him down. She plays tennis, does volunteer hospital work, and sews with a group of ladies who do fantastic things with needles, thread, and snippets of yarn.

And they've traveled: Bermuda each spring, Hawaii or the Caribbean in early December, Europe each fall. Their trip to Sarajevo this year for the Winter Olympics was a real experience. Each autumn, they close their trip visiting with friends in England. South America, Mexico, Canada, and Alaska have all been tested, and they always look for new acquaintances, antiques, and great meals.

Outstanding food, well prepared and served, to seek and find and relish — that's the challenge. They have eclectic tastes, not consistently gourmet: from brains and eggs in the Quaker House in Woodland, North Carolina (never on the menu), to fresh caviar in the home of an Iranian government official in Teheran (before the Ayatollah), to roast goose with the Noel-Hume's in Williamsburg.

Polly's home cooking keeps them both a little on the plump side, but they forget the calorie counting when they enjoy the tempting variety at E'toile in London; roast beef and Yorkshire Pudding at Simpson's on the Strand; the squid, octopus, and lobster in the Athens port of Piraeus; the shrimp tempura at Yamato's in Los Angeles; the fruits de mer in a small restaurant off St. Mark's Square in Venice; or month-old lamb enjoyed on a yacht cruising the Aegean Sea.

Now in their forty-first year of marriage, they know that friends, good food, and many other shared interests hold them together, just as Hampton Roads is the tangy mastic which bonds together the varied cities and counties of southeastern Virginia.

Susan and Peter Coe

Susan and Peter Coe are known in Hampton Roads as food and wine lovers extraordinaire. As owners of Taste Unlimited, a chain of five specialty food and wine stores in Norfolk and Virginia Beach, they have been trend-setters for years. Their shops are a timely cultural addition to an area rich in the culture of many nations.

The Coes' accomplishments in the area of food and wine have been widely recognized by the press; local and national interviews have been done, the most recent being a feature story in the Great Cooks section of *Bon Appétit* magazine.

Susan, born in Key West, Forida, has lived most of her life in Hampton Roads. She is active in many civic organizations and is the current chairman of Norfolk's XXXI International Azalea Festival. Known by her friends as an innovative, imaginative cook and baker, Susan enjoys creating new recipes and variations of old ones. Invitations to her multi-course Chinese banquets are coveted. At present she is editing and testing recipes for a cookbook by the Junior League of Norfolk and Virginia Beach. Peter, a Connecticut native, has lived in various parts of the country and abroad. Before starting Taste Unlimited, as an executive with a national corporation, his interest in food was stimulated as he spent his vacations working with his friend, the late Albert Stockli, chef and founder of the Four Seasons Restaurant in New York. Peter appears regularly on Hampton Roads television and radio programs doing cooking demonstrations and discussing different subjects on food and wine. When word comes out that he is having a wine tasting, seating quickly becomes hard to obtain. In addition, Peter is co-author of a nationally-distributed book on coffee and is in the planning stages for a new book.

The Coes enjoy traveling, taking at least one trip to Europe and one to California each year in search of new products and ideas for Taste Unlimited. They both think that the fun of dining in Hampton Roads is the variety of restaurants and their increased emphasis on locally-produced foods and locally-caught fish and seafood. The Coes are also delighted about the variety and quality of the wines that are appearing on the lists of the better Hampton Roads restaurants.

Ann and Cliff Cutchins

Hampton Roads and Virginia Beach have a special meaning for Ann and Cliff Cutchins. This is where they first met when their families were vacationing shortly after Cliff returned from active service in World War II.

Ann's sister asked her to "be nice" to Cliff because he had been an Eagle Scout in her husband's Boy Scout troop and had been raised on a farm in Southampton County. Subsequent events show that she more than complied with this request; they were married ten months later. Now their family numbers fifteen, including seven grandchildren.

Cliff's family originally came from Wales and settled in Virginia in the early 18th century. Ann's forebears were Scotch-Irish who settled in Pennsylvania in 1710; however, her mother was a Virginian. As coincidence would have it, Ann and Cliff's grandfathers were roommates in boarding school.

Cliff is an executive of a financial services corporation. The family moved to Norfolk in 1965 following a merger of two banks. He has been closely associated with several organizations in the health care field and has been active on several boards and committees of his alma mater, Virginia Tech. Cliff has continued his interest in agriculture and spends some of his free time with his diversified farming operation.

Ann has been active in several civic, cultural, and benevolent organizations in Norfolk. She loves to play tennis and frequently fits it into her schedule. Her principal pleasure is in bringing the families of her three sons together so that all can keep in close touch. She is especially eager for the cousins to know each other and to grow up together.

During the summer, Ann and Cliff may be found walking along the ocean at Virginia Beach. They enjoy watching the activity on the horizon as the large U.S. Naval vessels and merchant ships steam in and out of the harbor and, on breezy days, the ocean is dotted with the colorful sails of catamarans and other sailboats skimming along the surface.

The Cutchins translate their affection for the Hampton Roads cities by the sea into an appreciation for the special products of the sea, especially oysters, shrimp, and crabs. For special events, Ann and Cliff are sure to include seafood on the menu of the day.

Martha and Richard Davis

When Dick and Martha Davis were first introduced by a mutual friend during the 1960's, Martha commented that Dick seemed to be "so busy doing so many things." No statement could more accurately summarize the lives of Virginia's "Second Family." The Davis' waterfront home in Portsmouth, with its view of spectacular sunsets on the Elizabeth River, is filled with thousands of mementos of their busy lives.

He is a native and lifelong resident of Portsmouth, an achiever with wide ranging accomplishments in business, civic, and political affairs. He is president of a mortgage banking company and on the Board of Governors for the Mortgage Bankers of America, director of the organization that manages the Tidewater Tides baseball team, two-term mayor of the City of Portsmouth, former State Democratic Chairman, and now Lt. Governor of the Commonwealth of Virginia.

She is known for both her independence, great sense of humor, and her devotion to her husband and their three children. While family commitments come first, she is also an astute businesswoman and an active participant in community activities that include the Chrysler Museum, Maryview Hospital Auxiliary, Holiday House, and the Special Olympics.

Travel they have shared since their 1967 marriage in Mexico has brought them to virtually every American city for politics, baseball, and business meetings. Dinners at the White House, seafood at Fisherman's Wharf in San Francisco, brunch in the New Orlean's French Quarter, a luau in Honolulu, a glass of wine at the Plaza Hotel in New York, or a dinner at Trader Vic's in Atlanta—the Davises thoroughly enjoy new cities, world famous hotels, or evenings with friends at fine American restaurants. The diversity of their lives is reflected in the variety of good food they enjoy: Italian, French, Chinese, and American cuisine; fresh clams, lobster, oysters; and California and Virginia wines.

While some would find the constant travel fatiguing, the Davises approach their lives with zest, enthusiasm, and a sense of humor that has characterized all their past experiences and accomplishments. Their devotion to family, their commitment to community, and their sheer enjoyment of old and new friends has been enhanced by the experience of traveling throughout America. And yet, when all is said and done, there's no better place than home—together. Both have been known to say with great pride, "It's good to be back in Tidewater again."

Jacqueline and John Gounaris

It is only appropriate that Jackie and John Gounaris should be involved as participating authors to a book that deals with gourmet dining. On their very first date ten years ago, they had lunch at Locke-Obers, one of the oldest and finest restaurants in Boston. Gourmet dining has been one of their hobbies ever since that first date.

Relative newcomers to Hampton Roads, Jackie and John arrived in March 1983 from Chicago. Jackie is a native of Grosse Pointe, Michigan, and John was born in Boston and grew up in the nearby suburbs of Watertown and Medford, Massachusetts. In the spring of 1983, they bought a home in the Ghent Square area of Norfolk; however, since their new home would not be completely ready until late July, they lived in a two-room suite at the Omni International Hotel on Norfolk's waterfront and had reason to eat out in Hampton Road's restaurants just about every night for five months. It was this forced experience that opened their eyes to the outstanding variety of fine dining that exists in Southeastern Virginia.

It was John who first suggested that Hampton Roads be included in the series of *Dining In* cookbooks. In June of 1982, while coordinating the personal appearance of his friends, fashion designers Albert and Pearl Nipon, for a Chicago fashion benefit, John was given the book, *Dining In–Philadelphia*, as a gift from the author, Pearl Nipon. It was the first time he had seen her more excited about something other than fashion in the many years he had known her. The Philadelphia book started Jackie and John as collectors of the series of *Dining In* books and began the process of experiencing their favorite recipes at home. Cooking became a hobby for both of them, and their library boasts many of the *Dining In* series.

Jackie and John are both retail executives; he is president of Rices Nachmans, and she is merchandise manager with Added Dimensions, a division of Virginia Specialty Stores. They travel extensively, both on business and for pleasure. Their travels have taken them to Europe, to the Far East, and to every corner of the United States and Canada. In addition to gourmet dining, their hobbies include tennis (they are an avid mixed doubles team), biking, and skiing.

Thanks go to John Gounaris, for without his inspiration this book, and the proceeds from its sale which go to The Children's Hospital of the King's Daughters, would not have been possible.

Helen Anrod Jones and Alfred B. Rollins, Jr.

They eat out more than they care to admit, but not all of it is real. Much of it is road food: the much maligned chicken on the banquet circuit or sandwiches brought to assignment locations from the closest fast-food operation. As a university president and a free lance photographer, they often eat these meals separately, in varied locations and often alone. When they eat out for real—just the two of them—with time for conversation, hand holding, the joy of selecting good food and wine, they find themselves rejuvenated and pleasured by the experience.

They are relatively new to the Hampton Roads area. Al Rollins has been President of Old Dominion University since 1976, arriving via the University of Vermont, a long academic stint in New York state, and a New England childhood. Helen Anrod Jones has spent her career as a photographer in and out of American cities since 1972. She arrived as a new bride in a new town in 1981, fresh from New York City, with a history of other big city residences.

They both come from families where cooking was not perceived as an art form. "Meat and potatoes" were the norm. Their understanding and appreciation of fine food developed in spite of that, as their lives took the unexpected turns that have come with their adventuresome spirits and inquisitiveness about the world. One host or hostess after another who *did* practice the art of fine dining offered each of them experiences that sent them searching for more. The best of the gourmet places and ethnic restaurants became "collector items" as they traveled about.

Helen became curious as to "how" a meal reached fruition and embarked on learning "how to" in her own kitchen. Every city offered teachers. Italian restaurant owners in South Philadelphia explained the importance of knowing when to use the stem and when to use the leaves of parsley. In San Juan, Al Gomez, owner of Al's Little Club, watched over her shoulder, offering his critique, as she prepared her first paella, her first *tocino del cielo*, or her first perfect carmelized flan. The chefs at Rockefeller Resorts in the Caribbean where she worked discussed the nuance of sea grapes used in a salad dressing and the importance of not wasting anything in an environment where almost all food stuffs are imported.

Al is interested more in the results than in the process. He searches for the best restaurant offerings for himself and the many people he entertains while pursuing the interests of the University.

When they travel for pleasure rather than business, they head for France and Italy where the wonderful Mediterranean light, good food and exciting people create perfect experiences for them.

184

Eleanor and Robert Stanton

Having gone to one of the restaurants featured in *Dining In–Hampton Roads* (Lockhart's) on their first date, it is appropriate that the Stantons are a part of the editorial team. Traveling extensively and entertaining visitors to the Hampton Roads area has given them an opportunity to enjoy not only some of the finest restaurants in the world but virtually all of those featured in this volume.

Eleanor and Bob were both born in the Hampton Roads area and have spent their entire lives here. Eleanor is a Norfolk native being a descendant of an old Virginia family (the Tylers) whose family includes many famous Virginians. Her father was a member of the state's House of Delegates and is retired from his post as chairman of United Virginia Bank/Norfolk. Her grandfather on her mother's side of the family was Charles Burroughs, who was chairman of Royster Company and founder of Bayville Farms, two of Hampton Roads' most significant enterprises. Eleanor has maintained the family's tradition of community service and has served on the Board of Trustees of the Children's Hospital of The King's Daughters for many years. She is currently serving as president of the Board. She is also a member of the board of Norfolk Collegiate School.

Bob was born in Portsmouth and grew up in the Churchland area of that city. He attended college locally at Old Dominion University, graduating in 1961. He is one of the owners and serves as president of Goodman Segar Hogan, Inc., one of the largest commercial real estate companies in the country. His firm's interests range from owning office buildings in California to shopping centers in North Carolina. They recently built The World Trade Center in Norfolk. He has been active in industry affairs and has served on the Boards of various trade and professional organizations. Like Eleanor, Bob is active in community affairs. He is on the Board of Visitors of Old Dominion University and serves on the Executive Committe of Greater Norfolk Corporation. He served for nine years on the Board of Trustees for Norfolk Academy. He has been active in numerous other civic organizations and was named First Citizen of Virginia Beach in 1976.

The Stantons are in the process of building a new home at Bayville Farms in Virginia Beach. Together with other descendants of the farm's founder, Charles Burroughs, they have established a Holstein breeding operation at Bayville. Much of their spare time is committed to attending cattle auctions, visiting with other breeders, and developing their knowledge of the dairy industry.

Sally and Robert Sutton

Sally and Robert Sutton, being native Carolinians, searched for decades to find a dish better than Carolina barbeque. As any sophisticated gourmet should know, this is a difficult quest, and it carried the Suttons from couscous in Marrakesh to shabushabu in Kyoto. Fortunately, they found what they were looking for in Hampton Roads. The exciting and ever-changing variety of restaurants, with a concentration on preparing the abundantly available seafood, enabled the Suttons to control their barbeque dependency.

The Suttons met on a blind date while they were both students in college, she at Greensboro College and he at Davidson. They were married several years later while Bob was serving as an Air Force officer. The twenty-seven years of their marriage have produced a daughter (a Duke University student) and a son (a high school senior). They have lived in Cheyenne, Wyoming; New York City; Casablanca, Morocco; Chapel Hill and Charlotte, North Carolina; and, finally, they moved to Hampton Roads in 1968.

Sally, an accomplished musician, taught public school music and directed chorus in the early years of their marriage while Bob, a CPA, committed his career to Peat, Marwick, Mitchell & Co. He became managing partner of Peat Marwick's Norfolk office in 1968. The family has been actively involved in a broad range of activities in Hampton Roads. Sally served as president of her garden club, the Scherzo Music Club, her church choir, and on the board of the Virginia Orchestra League. She is now on the board of Young Audiences of Virginia. Meanwhile, Bob became an officer of his local CPA chapter, president of the Virginia Philharmonic and Virginia Pops, president of the Norfolk Chamber of Commerce, and chairman of the Hampton Roads Chamber of Commerce. With all this, they still have found time for travel across the United States, to the Caribbean, Hawaii, Japan, and Europe.

Sally and Bob Sutton have reached the stage in life when "eating out" is one of life's great pleasures (they probably reached that stage at age 20). The three things they value when dining are service, well-prepared food, and interesting atmosphere; the right setting transforms the first two into a memorable experience. Since much of the fascination of dining out in Hampton Roads revolves around seafood, they have enjoyed many a glass of white wine, including the excellent offerings from several Virginia vineyards. The Suttons' only complaint is that they did not arrive in Hampton Roads at a younger age when calories were as easily burned off as they were consumed.

Juanita and Eugene Walters

For Juanita and Gene Walters, their first meeting was at Finches, a drive-in restaurant in Spartanberg, South Carolina. Little did they suspect that, with a toss of a peach between convertibles, the "guy with the cute smile" and the "girl with the glorious eyes" would grow to become cuisine connoisseurs world-over.

Having both grown up on farms, they know the value of what "good" cooking really is. While serving in the infantry at Camp Croft, Spartenberg, South Carolina, Gene managed the officers' club. It was there that his palate was seasoned for dishes with class, quality, and good taste. Moreover, working in the food industry for over 35 years has taught the Walters the necessity of quality beginning ingredients.

Gene Walter's civilian work has brought them to every state in the United States and to many countries in every continent in the world except Australia. It is because of this traveling and exposure to all kinds of food that they have learned to appreciate what is considered "the best." Juanita chooses French and Hawaiian dishes as her most unique favorites and "always prefers a white Riesling wine" as a compliment. Gene prefers a "good western grain-fed steak with a bottle of red Domaine Chamguilliam." Along with knowing what to expect in fine cuisine, Gene knows how to get it. He is his own good chef and especially enjoys grilling turkeys and steaks. All-American dishes are Juanita's favorite in her own kitchen, too.

They agree that good food requires good service when dining out. They most enjoy small dinner parties in their home as well as in restaurants with masterful chefs who are willing to experiment. Good atmosphere is also essential to them, and their favorite restaurants are quaint ones which are small enough to be able to give special attention to their dinner guests.

RECIPE INDEX

Entrées

Salad Dressings

Salads

Sauces and Special Seasonings

Soups

Vegetables and Side Dishes

NOTES

NOTES

DINING IN–THE GREAT CITIES
A Collection of Gourmet Recipes from the Finest Chefs in the Country

Each book contains gourmet recipes for complete meals from the chefs of 21 great restaurants.

____ *Dining In–Baltimore* $7.95	____ *Dining In–Minneapolis/St. Paul, Vol. II* . $8.95
____ *Dining In–Boston (Revised)* 8.95	____ *Dining In–Monterey Peninsula* 7.95
____ *Dining In–Chicago, Vol. II* 8.95	____ *Dining In–Philadelphia* 8.95
____ *Dining In–Chicago, Vol. III* 8.95	____ *Dining In–Phoenix* 8.95
____ *Dining In–Cleveland* 8.95	____ *Dining In–Pittsburgh (Revised)* 7.95
____ *Dining In–Dallas (Revised)* 8.95	____ *Dining In–Portland* 7.95
____ *Dining In–Denver* 7.95	____ *Dining In–St. Louis* 7.95
____ *Dining In–Hampton Roads* 8.95	____ *Dining In–San Francisco, Vol.II (Fall'84)* . 8.95
____ *Dining In–Hawaii* 8.95	____ *Dining In–Seattle, Vol. III* 8.95
____ *Dining In–Houston, Vol. II* 7.95	____ *Dining In–Sun Valley* 7.95
____ *Dining In–Kansas City (Revised)* 8.95	____ *Dining In–Toronto* 8.95
____ *Dining In–Los Angeles (Revised)* 8.95	____ *Dining In–Vail (Fall '84)* 8.95
____ *Dining In–Manhattan* 8.95	____ *Dining In–Vancouver, B.C.* 8.95
____ *Dining In–Milwaukee* 8.95	____ *Dining In–Washington, D.C.* 8.95

☐ Check (✔) here if you would like to have a different Dining In–Cookbook sent to you once a month. Payable by MasterCard or VISA. Returnable if not satisfied.

☐ Payment enclosed $ _____ (Please include $1.00 postage and handling for each book)

☐ Charge to:

VISA # _____ Exp. Date _____

MasterCard # _____ Exp. Date _____

Signature _____

Name _____

Address _____

City _____ State _____ Zip _____

SHIP TO (if other than name and address above):

Name _____

Address _____

City _____ State _____ Zip _____

PEANUT BUTTER PUBLISHING
911 Western Avenue, Suite 401, Maritime Building ▪ Seattle, WA 98104 ▪ (206) 628-6200

HR 5/84